THE GREAT MYSTERIES

THE GREAT
MYSTERIES

EXPERIENCING CATHOLIC FAITH
from the INSIDE OUT

ANDREW M. GREELEY

SHEED & WARD

Lanham • Chicago • New York • Toronto • Plymouth, UK

Published by Sheed & Ward
An imprint of the Rowman & Littlefield Publishing Group, Inc.
A wholly owned subsidiary of the Rowman & Littlefield Publishing Group, Inc.
4501 Forbes Boulevard, Suite 200, Lanham, Maryland 20706
Distributed by National Book Network

The hardback edition of this book was previously cataloged by the
Library of Congress as follows:

Greeley, Andrew M., 1928–
    The great mysteries : experiencing Catholic faith from the inside out /
    Andrew M. Greeley.
        p. cm.
Includes bibliographical references.
    ISBN 1-58051-131-7 (alk. paper)
    1. Theology, Doctrinal—popular works. 2. Theology, Catholic. I. Title.
    BT77.G837 2003
    230'.2—dc21

                                                          2003006023

ISBN-13: 978-1-58051-220-6 (pbk. : alk. paper)
ISBN-10: 1-58051-220-8 (pbk. : alk. paper)

Printed in the United States of America

∞™ The paper used in this publication meets the minimum requirements of
American National Standard for Information Sciences—Permanence of Paper for
Printed Library Materials, ANSI/NISO Z39.48-1992.

Contents

FOREWORD

God's Great "Yes"

T HE CATHOLIC THEOLOGIAN HANS URS VON BALTHASAR SAID that the greatest tragedy in the history of Christianity was neither the Crusades nor the Reformation nor the Inquisition, but rather the split that opened up between theology and spirituality at the end of the Middle Ages. In the early centuries of the Church's life, the most influential theologians were not academics in our sense of the term, but rather pastors, catechists, bishops, and spiritual directors. They wrote, not for tenure or for publication in learned journals, but to doctor souls. If you had asked Augustine, Chrysostom, Jerome, or even Thomas Aquinas to distinguish between his theology and his spirituality, he wouldn't have understood the question.

But this changed around the year 1300 when theology became exclusively a university discipline and spirituality branched off as a separate concern of monks and mystics. For Balthasar, this disjunction proved disastrous for both sides, giving rise to a theology void of life and a spirituality too often void of substance. And what it produced by the middle of the twentieth century, during the years when Andrew Greeley was coming of age, was a dryly propositional

and uninspiring catechetics. When he was a seminary student at
Mundelein during the late 1940's and early 1950's, Greeley was
bored by the scholastic manuals that were the standard academic
fare, and he used clandestinely to read the works of the proponents
of the so-called "new theology"—Jean Danièlou, Pierre Teilhard de
Chardin, Yves Congar, and especially Henri de Lubac. All of these
theologians were, like Balthasar, eager to repair the rift between
technical theology and what Greeley would come to call "experience,"
life concretely lived. In many ways, The Great Mysteries is Andrew
Greeley's tribute to these figures who proved so influential at the
Second Vatican Council and whose vision fired him as a young man.
It is his attempt to respond to the call of that great generation of
theologians to re-attach faith and life, doctrine and experience.

The Great Mysteries is also deeply indebted to Greeley's favorite philosopher, the nineteenth-century Irish-American William
James. Throughout his career, James cultivated an intense dis-
like of Hegelian and Platonic abstractions and insisted that true
knowledge is had through a radical immersion in the ever-changing
and evolving stream of experience that he termed "the blooming,
buzzing confusion." Like James, Greeley is a radical empiricist,
preferring the untidy, sweaty, particular truth of things to pristine
generalizations. And so in his catechism, his concern is to enter
into the stream of religious experience—tasting, testing, compar-
ing, experimenting and wondering. To be sure, he is guided in the
process by doctrine, but, like John Henry Newman (another of
his heroes), he stubbornly wants generalities to serve particulars
and not vice versa.

In some ways, the two approaches I have just outlined—
de Lubac's and James's—come together in Greeley's love for nar-
rativity. While a concept can state a truth thinly and universally,
a story can show it "thickly," which is to say specifically, colorfully
and in its multi-faceted complexity. As such, a story can sing the
truth and not just tell it, eliciting in the hearer not only an intellectual response, but also a deeply emotional engagement. Greeley

maintains in this introduction to *The Great Mysteries*, that religion is action-oriented since it shapes "our way of doing everything." But as Newman knew, though universals can delight and inform the mind, only particulars—this face, that voice, this person, that story—can move the heart to action and commitment. It seems to me that Greeley adopted a narrative strategy in *The Great Mysteries* because he wanted to affect a change, not only in the reader's mind, but in her life.

I first read this catechism when I was seventeen, and I was struck then by the sense of vitality that runs through it. In Greeley's vision, God is an agent of life and life to the full. Even (perhaps especially) when we run toward death, God runs around us, heads us off at the pass, and displays new possibilities for growth and flourishing. When I re-read these pages not long ago—with my somewhat older eyes—I saw this same theme under the rubric of the divine providence. Thomas Aquinas said that the word "God" names an operation, by which he meant the gracious providence which governs and directs the world, bringing it safely home. When religious people speak of the "Absolute," the "Infinite," the "Totally Other," "God," they mean, not so much a distant cosmic force or unmerciful moral judge, as this love that lurks (one of Greeley's favorite words) behind all things, pushing, pulling, and cajoling them.

The "lurking" God is also the ground of the sacramentalism that is evident on practically every page of *The Great Mysteries*. Throughout his career, Greeley has complained about an either/or form of thinking that has, periodically, haunted the Christian imagination: the soul or the body, thought or feeling, the supernatural or the natural, God or the world. At its best, Catholicism has repudiated this kind of dualism and has opted for the both/and, analogical style: body in the soul and soul in the body, feeling as a modality of thought, the natural suffused with the supernatural, God available in and through creation. Nowhere is this metaphysics of co-inherence more apparent than in the greatest of all Christian doctrines, the Incarnation. In light of Jesus Christ, we simply *have* to say God *and* the world, grace *and* nature. And this is why Greeley's Catholic Christian catechism is relentlessly analogical, or if you prefer, sacramental.

Another theme that especially struck me when I re-read this text is that of the struggle. In chapter after chapter, Greeley insists upon the darkness of the cosmos and the tragic elements in human life: sickness, depression, broken relationships, disasters, upheavals in nature, death itself. Despite its exuberant sacramentalism, there is nothing naïve or blindly "optimistic" about Greeley's vision. It is a commonplace of the Bible that the spiritual life is a sort of warfare. In the book of Genesis, God's spirit hovers over the surface of the chaotic waters. These waters—which re-appear as Noah's flood, the Red Sea blocking the Israelites' escape, the stormy lake of Galilee—stand for all those forces that are opposed to God's creative intentions. Yet, the story that God tells is finally, as Dante knew, a divine comedy. Time and again in *The Great Mysteries*, Greeley interprets Christianity as the proclamation of light in the midst of darkness, final victory after many losses, life trumping death. Life is a struggle, but we know, in Christ, that God will win.

James Joyce's greatest novel ends with the musings of Molly Bloom. In her rambling life review, she says, over and over again, "yes," and her final word, the closing word of the whole book, is "Yes." This, for Andrew Greeley, is the authentic voice of the Holy Spirit, the creator and redeemer, the providential guide who lures us, often despite ourselves, to life. What he sees in all Christian doctrine—creation, redemption, Christology, Mariology, Trinity, cross and resurrection—is God's exuberant, child-like, irrepressible "Yes."

For this light-filled interpretation of Christianity, we should all give thanks.

—REV. ROBERT BARRON

INTRODUCTION

RELIGION IS GROUNDED IN HUMAN EXPERIENCE. IN THE MIDST of the frustrations, the ambiguities, the sorrows, the pleasures, the joys, the uncertainties of our lives, we occasionally sense that there may be something else going on. For some people, this "something else" is encountered in a dramatic, overpowering, ecstatic way. But for most of us it is perceived briefly and dimly: in the smile on a child's face, the glory of a sunset, or a day of pleasure and joy with good friends. At such times we feel at one with ourselves, nature, and humanity. We know, of course, that the smile will vanish from the child's face, the sun will set and darkness will cover the earth, and our friends will go home, leaving us alone. We know that our perceptions of good things will end with our own death; but in that fleeting glimpse of the possibility of "something else" being at work in the world, we get a hint—sometimes faint and sometimes very strong—that there is something else in the universe besides our own brief and fragile life. It is out of these hints that humankind fashions religion.

There are different names to describe this Something Else: the Sacred, the Ultimate, the Transcendent, the Other, and, in a marvelous burst of German existentialist redundancy, the Totally Other. But whatever we call that phenomenon that flits across our preoccupied, mundane consciousness, religion is that kind of human activity that attempts to relate our life to the Something Else that may be at work in the universe. The most basic of religious questions—maybe the only one that really matters—is whether we can accept the claim to graciousness and loving care that the Something Else seems to be making in our occasional encounter with it.

There have been some extraordinarily powerful and intense experiences of the Something Else down through human history. From these special events come the great religious traditions, which attempt to share these very special experiences with those who "were not there." A wandering collection of desert nomads became aware of their common peoplehood at the foot of a mountain, and in that awareness experienced the graciousness of the God who, on his own initiative, entered into a covenant with them that constituted them a people. The rest of Jewish religious history consists of efforts to keep alive the memory of the Sinai experience so that those who were not there could encounter the love and goodness of the gracious Lord of Sinai.

Similarly, a group of Galilean peasants, fishermen, and tradesmen developed an extraordinary relationship with a very special kind of popular preacher. Much to their sorrow, he did not establish the temporal kingdom everyone expected. He was arrested and executed by the soldiers of the occupying power. But to their complete astonishment, his followers did experience him as supremely alive after he died. In the power of that Easter experience of the risen Lord they came to understand, as they never had done previously, what he was talking about when he preached. They perceived him as a special messenger of God who preached, more strongly than anyone ever had before, the great intensity and intimacy of the Something Else's love for humankind. Indeed, they saw that the Something Else—God—was present in Jesus in a unique and special way so that he was God's son in a way others were not.

They saw that life did matter, that God did love his creatures, that death was not the end, and that with the coming of Jesus a new era in human history had begun. Humankind was getting a second chance, a fresh new start. Filled with enthusiasm and excitement over this experience—which ran contrary to the fears and insecurities of their own personalities—they immediately went forth to share the Good News of their experience with the rest of humankind.

Thus came Christianity.

It rose out of the Easter experience of the apostles: Jesus who had been crucified was still alive. He was the "Christ," the chosen one of God. And it was about the "Christ experience" that the apostles began to preach. They wanted others to share in their experience and to see that God, by protecting his beloved son from death, had validated, confirmed, reinforced, ratified the Good News that Jesus had preached. Note well two things about the early preaching of the followers of Jesus, for these two things tell us much about religion, specifically the religion that emerged from the Christ experience.

First of all, their preaching was not aimed at winning converts. They did not use elaborate or sophisticated arguments. (Although there were traces of such arguments even in their early preaching. Humans are philosophical animals, and their need to ask philosophical questions can never be denied.) Rather they tried to share their experience with others. They wanted their listeners to experience the risen Jesus the way they had. If they could communicate the Christ experience, that was enough. So they used pictures, stories, and images more than they used arguments. They tried to appeal to the Something Else experiences of their audiences so that they could show how their Christ experience validated and confirmed and enormously enriched all the experiences of hope and joy and love and celebration that everyone has. Like all religious preachers, the apostles quickly learned that you must call out of the recesses of emotional memory the experiences of others in order for them to be able to share in your experience. You do not argue as much as you tell stories, draw pictures, stir up images so that you can touch the depths of the religious creativity that is at work constantly—if often only peripherally—in the consciousness of others.

Secondly, the apostles were not teaching speculative or theoretical knowledge. They were not interested in teaching metaphysical, scientific, or historical knowledge of the sort that people would later treat in learned dissertations. Their concerns were preeminently practical. They wanted people to change their lives by experiencing the risen Jesus, the one who had already transformed the lives of the apostles themselves. And this transformation was not primarily an intellectual or speculative matter at all—though since it was a thoroughly human event, the intellect was by no means absent. The Easter experience, the Christ event, showed humans how to live because it explained to them what life means and of what the Something Else is which underpins life.

All religious knowledge, then, is practical before it becomes speculative. In time it becomes the basis for that elaborate and complex religious reflection called theology. Theological activity begins very early, however; necessarily, because as humans we must reflect and speculate at every step. Religious knowledge is practical, but not because it ordinarily provides a detailed program for human living; such programs evolve only with time, and not infrequently stray far from the insight of the original religious experience. It is practical because it illuminates the most basic and dense agonies that torment human life; it speaks to us of good and evil, life and death, love and hate, hope and tragedy. If one can cope with those terrible uncertainties, the problems of daily life begin to fall into place; but if the chaos implicit in those uncertainties cannot be held in check, we live our daily lives poised perilously close to the brink of absurdity and despair. Religion is practical because it tells us how to live. It tells us how to live by explaining what our life means.

In this book, which is written as a catechism for our times—a way of exploring Catholic faith from the inside out rather than from the outside in—I take a dozen of the images, pictures, and stories that have traditionally been used to communicate the apostles'

Easter experience of the risen Jesus, and show that light can be shed on the basic dilemmas of our existence if we permit ourselves to share the Christ experience the first Christians had. My starting point is not creedal or dogmatic statements of the Catholic faith; rather, I begin in human experience, in the story of our lives, and put these stories and experiences in dialogue with the richness of the Catholic faith tradition.

It will be argued that this is a revolutionary and perhaps dangerous new approach to catechetics. It is not. On the contrary, it is a return to the form of religious instruction that has been characteristic of most of Catholic history. The technique of this catechism may be a striking departure from the catechetics—conciliar or even post-conciliar—that we have come to take for granted; but those catechetical approaches most of us remember from childhood years were very untraditional—however useful they may have been in that time and in those circumstances.

Religious knowledge and religious teaching are both experiential and practical. One need only read the New Testament to confirm that truth. But our catechisms for the last century or so have been abstract, theoretical, and speculative. They have addressed themselves to complex metaphysical, scientific, historical, and ethical issues that go far beyond that religious knowledge that stirs up in us an experience of the Other and tells us what human life means.

In principle one cannot object to abstract religious speculation as long as the basic practical and experiential aspect of religious knowledge is given primary emphasis; but the catechisms and the religious education they represent have got so bogged down in speculative discussion that they produce, not a re-experience of the Easter joy but, if anything, the experience of Peter, James, and John falling asleep in the Garden of Olives.

How many times, for example, we have heard someone say: "Do you still believe in the divinity of Jesus?" or "I can no longer accept the divinity of Jesus," or "My big problem with Christianity is that I'm not sure whether Jesus was God."

Note what has happened. A truth of faith has become an intellectual matter that is either the subject of an examination to determine whether one is orthodox, a barrier that must be surmounted before one can join the Christian community, or a doubt about which one can endlessly agonize.

That is not, I would submit, what religion is all about. The proper question is not "What do we have to believe?" but rather "What light is shed on the uncertainties and agonies of human existence by the experience-producing pictures, stories, and images of our faith?"

I do not wish to suggest that it is pointless to worry over the metaphysical problem of how humanity and divinity are combined in a special way in Jesus. Christians have philosophized over that question since the beginning—without ever coming up with a completely satisfactory answer, be it noted. But I would contend that the basic religious question about Jesus is not "How is he different from the rest of us?" but "Can I live in the gloriously joyous world view that Jesus came to share with us and that Christianity claims to have validated in the experience of the Easter event?"

Such a question does not represent a watering down of faith. It does not try to make religion palatable to modern scientific empiricism by eliminating all wonder and mystery. On the contrary, it is much easier to make an intellectual assent to the special presence of the deity in Jesus than it is to accept and conform our lives to the world view that Jesus represents.

This "new" approach to catechetics—to teaching the Catholic faith—is not easy to sell. Many Catholics were raised in an environment where metaphysical, abstract, and speculative questions were the most important ones. They are reluctant to give them up or to postpone considering them until they understand the Christian vision from the inside. Since one can understand a vision from the inside only by living it, the insistence that intellectualizing must come *before* instead of *after* commitment precludes the possibility of commitment, which actually seems to suit many people just fine.

However, the preaching of the apostles, as well as the whole of human religious history, shows that one can reflect on religious experience only after internalizing the experience itself. Catechetics, which we thought to be traditional, put the cart before the horse.

And under those circumstances, not surprisingly, the cart didn't move at all.

This catechism, then, assumes that reflection and speculation will come after one has experienced the Christian vision from the inside, after one has permitted the truths of the Christian faith to illumine and direct one's life. But there is a major difference between contemporary humans and their predecessors of apostolic times, who were convinced by the story (or the picture or the image). It did not have to be analyzed or interpreted in any great detail to provide acceptable answers to the great questions that plague human life. We live in a far more analytic age. We ask not merely what life means but what the stories that purport to explain life mean. Before, during, and after we share in the great experiences which formed our religious tradition, we must have explicit interpretations of the meaning of those experiences. We must take them apart, analyze them, "unpack" them so that we can examine every detail of their meaning.

Hence this is a catechism of interpretation. Its goal is not to argue, not to persuade, not to provide abstract and speculative theories, but rather to explain how the central truths of the Christian tradition purport to explain the human condition for those who permit them to do so. There is more speculation and theory in this book than in the New Testament, because we are a far more theoretical people than our predecessors, and our interpretations need to be much more detailed than theirs. But we are still plagued with the same questions about the meaning of human life that plagued them. We must, if we are to be Christians, experience the responses to those questions that the Christ event elicited from them.

So far I have called the means by which this experience is communicated "stories, images, and pictures" or "truths of the faith." The first series is awkward and the second phrase can easily be taken in an abstract and theoretical sense (though it need not be so understood). Two better words, which come from the same Latin and Greek word, are "symbol" and "mystery." By "symbol" I do not mean *only* a symbol; I mean a story that tells us what human life means. By "mystery" I do not mean something that is hard to cope with because it is obscure and baffling; I mean something that is hard to cope with because it is so bright and dazzling. To say that the resurrection of Jesus is a symbol does not mean that Jesus did not really rise from the dead; it means rather that his resurrection is a story (and in therewith and Christian religions, since they are historical, almost all the meaning-giving stories must be based on historical fact). It tells us something very important about the meaning of human life; it tells us that we will all survive death—a fact far more astonishing than the survival of one man who died.

The Greek word from which "symbol" and "mystery" come can also be translated as "secret." St. Paul is frequently translated as speaking of the great "secret" hidden from the ages and revealed in the Lord Jesus.

One can then speak of truth of faith, mystery of faith, symbol of faith, secret of faith, or even revelation of faith. The reader may choose. I use "mystery" because many readers will find it very hard to wrestle themselves free from the "only a symbol" meaning; for the same reasons I will use the word "reveals" instead of "symbolizes."

This catechism is deliberately short. Many readers are frightened off by a long catechism. I believe that one ought to be able to interpret the principal mysteries of Christianity and describe what they reveal to us in a relatively brief number of words—not too many more than in the Gospel stories themselves. Hence I am making no attempt to be comprehensive, to cover all the doctrines that must be believed under pain of mortal sin. The reader will note that I say nothing on the much controverted subject of papal infallibility. The reason for this omission is not that I reject the doctrine but that, despite all the controversy that has raged around it during the last hundred years, it is not at the absolute dead center of the Catholic tradition. The Church was able to survive without its explicit formulation for eighteen centuries, and while infallibility may be important, it is not nearly as important as resurrection. To put the matter differently, the doctrine of infallibility may rekindle the Easter experience and the Christ event for some people, but its potential for doing so is limited, I think. It may be a mystery, but it is not one of the great mysteries, and hence can safely be left to other and longer volumes.

I have tried, however, to include all the great mysteries, the core revelatory images of the Christian tradition. To say the same thing from another direction, I have tried to ask the basic questions of human life to see what light Christianity can throw on the frightening uncertainties that plague our temporal and fragile existence. I have not constrained the organization of this book on any particular order, for we do not progress down a direct path of logically arranged truths; rather we circle around the same poignant question: For example, we ask, What, if anything, does my life mean? I examine that question in the light of the Christ event as it is reflected in the great mysteries of the Catholic Christian heritage.

There will necessarily be overlapping among the chapters. A perfect diamond reflects and refracts intensified light from its facets as one inspects it from different angles; it is not revealed in all its richness from only one perspective. Yet no matter what way one turns the precious stone, it is still the same diamond. Thus it is with the mysteries of the Christ event; it is one encounter with God viewed from many different angles.

Religion, as I have defined it, is action-oriented; the religious experience impels humankind to act, and only later to reflect on the sudden burst of illuminating insight. The apostles encountered the risen Lord in the Easter experience and then went forth to preach. Only in time did they begin to seek out categories to explain and articulate what had happened in that encounter. These categories were simple at first and then became more subtle and complex. But religion is not a system of ethics. Religion responds to the basic and ultimate anxieties of human life, and by so doing paints a broad picture of how the good person lives. Most religious traditions adopt ethical systems, developed either by their own members or out of their pagan heritage. Ethical systems fill in the details, sometimes at the cost of obscuring the broad picture. There is an extremely powerful and comprehensive ethical demand in the Christ event: we must love and serve others as God loves and serves us. Those who are caught up in the joy of Easter must bear that joy to others by his loving and happy care of them.

However useful and necessary ethical systems may be, and however much they run the risk of turning the spirit of the law into its letter, they are not the same as religion. A systematic ethics may be derived from religious insight, although the various attempts to do so during the last two thousand years have not always been successful. The point is that these systems are derivative and no substitute either for the ethical demand that is at the core of the original Christ event or for a decision to respond to that demand. Hence in the present volume there will be rather little about systematic moral obligations—though these are by no means unimportant. Christianity is not an ethical system but a response to the Christ event, a response that reorders our life both toward the Something Else and toward all the "someone elses" with whom we share the planet.

The readers who seek reassurance in this catechism from the rote repetition of the answers they learned mechanically as children will be disappointed. They should not conclude that the book is lacking in orthodoxy. I intend to deny nothing; I seek, rather, to interpret some of the core truths of faith. My approach may be useful to some and not useful to others. Those who do not find it useful would save great strain on their blood pressure if they simply discarded it now.

Those who find it useful may conclude that despite the imperfections that mark any tentative beginning, this catechism points the way back to the religious education of the past and forward to the religious education of the future.

That this book has been in print off and on over the past twenty years and is now updated and published by Sheed & Ward in the new millennium is gratifying, if only for the fact that I wrote it for all people at all times who ask new questions, live deeply, and are open to religious truth. I thank John Shea for recommending that I write this book in the first place and to Fr. John Cusick for suggesting to my editor, Jeremy Langford, that it is just as relevant today as ever. My aim is to take seriously life's questions and, instead of applying religious truths to life, search in life for hints that point at religious truth. I stand with the theologians who believe in the power of story, who see narrative as the fundamental, primordial, and most effective way to communicate a religious tradition. When I turned to writing novels, the correlations between religious symbols and human experience outlined in this book became for my novels the structure, the warp and the woof of the stories that I would tell. My greatest prayer is that you, modern reader, will use this book as a launching pad for your own questions and journey into the heart of faith. Amen.

—ANDREW M. GREELEY
EASTER 2003

Chapter One

THE MYSTERY OF GOD

Is there any purpose in my life?

(Why did God make me?)[1]

T HERE ARE TIMES WHEN OUR LIVES SEEM TO DRAG ON aimlessly, pointlessly. When we are young we are filled with enthusiasm and vigor, and we are less likely to be aware of the emptiness that lurks just below the surface of our great plans and our passionate pleasures. Those over thirty know beyond doubt what the young perceive but dimly: we are all dying. Time goes more quickly, summers are shorter, the years roll around more rapidly, we are not as vigorous as we used to be, and our energies and strengths and ambitions begin to weaken. The body does not respond the way it once did.

We watch the death notices more carefully, and we find ourselves attending more wakes and funerals. We are growing old, and death is much nearer than it was only a year ago. We had hoped for so much, we had expected so much, we had such bright dreams; now all that seems left is to grow older and then die.

We try to pretend to ourselves and to others that we are "as young as we ever were," but the pretense is hollow. Our lives, which looked so long in anticipation, look very short in retrospect. We accomplished so little, and now it is almost over. What was it all about? Why bother to live at all? What was the point of the whole collection of events that was us?

Life is filled with so many senseless events. Mindless tragedies fill our newspapers every day—airplane crashes, the murder of innocent children, insane terrorism, natural disasters. And much in our own lives seems without purpose or meaning—a rainstorm on a picnic or parade day, a bad cold when we are having a party, a disabled child, the early death of a parent or spouse, a broken marriage, a car that won't start in the morning, a wrong number in the middle of the night, the loss of savings through inflation or depression or corporate scandal, the misunderstandings and needless hurts of family life, the treason of friends, the envy of neighbors. Such tragedies, some large and some very small, seem to be without pattern or intent. Why do they happen?

Life, too, seems devoid of intent and purpose. Why does it happen?

Some scientists tell us that the whole universe is merely the result of random chance operating among atoms. About such an issue most of us are not much concerned, but when we look at our own daily, weekly, monthly, and yearly existence, such randomness and purposelessness is disturbing. When we were very young we thought we could plan our lives. Now we know that plans—large or small—almost always go awry. If there is any plan at all to our existence—and it is by no means clear that there is—then it must be Someone Else's plan.

We try not to ask these questions about meaning very often. We try not to wonder about purpose and chaos because the question is so large and so frightening. It is much easier to go about the daily tasks of eating and drinking, working and raising children, paying the bills or not being able to pay them, occasionally relaxing. Then we don't have time to worry about meaning and purpose; but the question still weighs heavy. Is life really "a tale told by an idiot, full of sound and fury, signifying nothing" as Shakespeare's Macbeth cries out? Is it really a meaningless interlude caught between two oblivions? Are we really subject to mindless, impersonal forces that care not at all about us? Are we really alone?

It often seems to be so. Life is mindless, purposeless, random, absurd. We live out our days, trying to keep our heads above water, and then it all comes to an end and we are quickly forgotten. So let us eat, drink, and be merry, for tomorrow or the next day or surely the day after we will die.

And yet . . . and yet we wish it were not so. There is in the depths of the human personality a stubborn and ineradicable conviction that our existence does have meaning and purpose no matter how problematic or obscure that purpose may be. We are caught between the seeming mindless arbitrary cruelty that we see all around us and this intractable conviction of purpose, which will not go away even when we are convinced that it is nothing more than self-deception.

Occasionally we think we have seen glimpses of what that purpose may be. For some people these glimpses are extraordinarily powerful. For a few brief moments the universe seems to flood into their personality, time stands still, and they feel they are lifted out of themselves, able to see the unity of the cosmos and their own place in it. Light, heat, warmth pour into them and they emerge with the unshakable conviction that everything will be all right.

Such experiences, in which conviction from without speaks overwhelmingly to conviction from within, are not so rare as we once thought. Still, two-thirds of our number do not have them; yet we all catch occasional flashes that shake us out of the dull routine, the ordered chaos, the noisy desperation of every day—and they make us wonder.

And wonder is the name of the game. It can be as elaborate as for the theoretical physicist who remarked that whatever is responsible for the universe seems to have known a lot of complex mathematical formulas long before we did. It can be as complicated as for the scientist pondering the immensity of space through which the light we see now has traveled since before the earth began; or as for the chemist realizing that inner space is filled with a dizzying array of tiny particles so small that if the atom were the size of the Milky Way, these particles would be smaller than the earth by comparison. Wonder can be as for the anthropologist realizing that if the age of the earth were one year, humankind appeared four hours before midnight on December 31, and civilization appeared just a half second before the stroke of midnight.

Or wonder can be as simple as a glimpse of a starry sky at night, the smell of spring returning for another year, the rushing of a brook through a forest, the joy of exquisite pleasure with one's spouse, the rose and gold rays of sunset, returning to where we grew up. Every interlude of wonder, simple or complex, forces upon us the same question: How come?

The words are the same whether we ask them in times of weariness, disappointment, frustration, tragedy; or in times of joy, insight, contentment. But with an experience of wonder they take on a totally different connotation. Then we are trying to explain, not absurdity but an intimation of graciousness, a hint that beyond the limits there is something else. Why the beautiful mathematical relationships? Why space—inner and outer? Why time and our place in its continuum? Why the sky, the forest, the rushing brook, the sunset, our lover's body? Why our moral sense? Why our urge to self-realization?

Why anything at all? Now we can ask in awe.

God is humankind's attempt to explain experiences of wonder and the awe that results from them. Since the wonder experiences hint that whatever is at work in the universe is both purposeful and gracious, God, we assume, is the purposeful and gracious one who is responsible for the universe and for our life.

There are many possible different interpretations of who God is; for humans must wrestle with the paradox of the graciousness and purpose they occasionally experience and the evil and absurdity that seem so typical of life. Fundamentally, religion is an attempt to harmonize graciousness and evil. God is the center of religion, and our image of God summarizes our response to the puzzle of absurdity and graciousness, of chance and awe.

Some versions see God as benign but forgetful; humans must remind God of his promises and sometimes wake him up from his sleep (Egyptian). Others see God as crotchety and difficult, easily offended by those who violate his plan, and quick to take salutary vengeance; humans must constantly placate and calm him (Babylonian). Still others think that God is fundamentally uninterested in the universe he has created, leaving its governance to irrational, or at least nonrational, forces he has set in motion (Greek and modern deism). And still others find substitute gods in the pursuit of freedom or social justice or a better life for all here on earth—a pursuit that is usually seen as part of some inevitable forward movement of humanity and acts as a substitute for a divine plan (Marxism, scientism).

It was to tell us about his God that Jesus came. At the core of the Christian experience of Jesus is an experience of the God Jesus claimed to represent in an absolutely unique and special way. And—one must say it with all due reverence—the God of Jesus is Something Else altogether. He is the same God the Jewish people encountered at Sinai—the God who on his own initiative entered into covenant with his people, the God who liberated his people from slavery and oppression, the God who passionately loved his people as a husband loves a wife even when she is faithless. He is the absolute Lord of all creation on which all other powers and forces are dependent; yet when he said in the Sinai experience "I am Yahweh, your God," he made covenant with his people. Uninvited, unasked, and frequently unwelcome and unwanted, Yahweh still made a commitment to his people, and he would remain implacably faithful to that commitment, whatever might come. He had freed them from slavery in Egypt, brought them through the waters of the Red Sea, led them by a pillar of cloud by day and a pillar of fire by night. He committed himself to give them their own land and then the whole world. In return he demanded their faithful love. He was a jealous and passionate God; he did not want a faithless or frigid people who went whoring off after false gods, but he would be faithful to his people whatever they did.

So the experiences of Exodus and Sinai produced for the Hebrews an encounter with a Gracious Purpose, which they perceived as unilaterally liberating His people and then entering into a passionately loving commitment to them. The Lord of the universe had sought them out, freed them, and then yoked Himself irrevocably to them. It was an incredibly daring and even outrageous notion of God, for it argued that the purpose of the universe could be described as a passionately loving and liberating commitment to a people.

The early Hebrews saw Yahweh as making a covenant with the whole people, but as time went on, their religious thinking developed and they perceived that Yahweh was in fact committing himself not only to the people but also to individual persons. He passionately loved each individual. The plan and purpose of life, then, as experienced and wondered at by the prophets, was a love affair freely entered into by the Lord of the universe with the individual human person. Whatever evil might occur, and however unfaithful the person might be, God's implacably faithful and passionate love would still be there.

Life, then, in the Hebrew worldview, was a response to a love already freely given and never to be withdrawn. Whatever defects this articulation of the wonder experience may have had, it was certainly not lacking in optimism. The God of the Hebrews may be too good to be true, but at least He is a God who is worth believing in. The universe may not be animated by passionate love, but it would be nice if it were. The graciousness we experience in times of wonder and awe may not be all that gracious, but surely it could not be more gracious than the Hebrews thought it was.

Jesus was very much a product of the religious currents of his time—however far he may have gone beyond those currents. He insisted that the rigid legalism that had grown up in the relationship between God and his people was absurd. You didn't earn God's love; it was a free gift to be responded to by a free gift of everything that one was and had. Jesus also believed, as we shall see in the next question, that in him and with his coming a new and decisive phase in God's relations with humans had begun. Jesus' followers would think of him as the new Adam, a re-creation of what was essential, a new humanity, a new Moses presiding over a new exodus of liberation and a new Sinai covenant. God in Jesus was renewing his passionate commitment to his people—now not merely a collectivity but a community of individual persons. While Jesus may not have used this precise terminology, there is no doubt that he believed that in him a new age of the world had begun.

Essential to the beginning of this new age was a deeper and qualitatively new insight into the depths of God's love. We can begin to grasp this insight if we look at the parables of Jesus. Here is where we are in most intimate contact with his worldview. It is especially in the parables that Jesus shares with us his own wonder experience of his heavenly Father. Two parables will suffice—the story of the crazy farmer and the story of the loving father (or, as we inappropriately call the latter, the Prodigal Son).

The men the farmer hired at the last hour of the day were loafers who, because they were lazy, lounged around the marketplace during harvest time when the work was plentiful. They probably did very little work in the short time they were in the fields. They were so ill-tempered that they were prepared to argue with the farmer if he didn't pay them enough. Much to their astonishment, they got a whole day's wage for doing virtually nothing. In the traditional parable, with which the crowds who listened to Jesus were quite familiar, the workers of the eleventh hour became so industrious that they did in one hour what it took others all day to do. They earned every cent of their pay. But Jesus turned the tables. The emphasis in his story is not on the industry of the workers but on the mad generosity of the farmer. No landowner, no matter how wealthy, can stay in business very long if he gives money away to those who do almost nothing.

The point of Jesus' parable is that by human standards the loving generosity of God is mad, lunatic, and insane.

The critical scene in the story of the loving father is the picture of the father rushing down the road to greet the errant son, cutting short his prepared speech of reproach with an embrace, clothing the astonished young man in new garments, and dragging him off to a feast of celebration. The young man deserved nothing. He was a spoiled brat, a rich man's wasteful son who ought to have been made to earn every inch of the way back into his father's favor. A father who continues to spoil such a ne'er-do-well will get only what he deserves when the son deserts him again.

Once again, the passionately loving generosity of God must appear bizarre to our careful, rational, human calculations.

It is not an exaggeration, then, but simply a literal interpretation of his parables to say that the God of Jesus is madly, insanely in love with his human creatures. Does my life have any purpose at all? The response of Christianity is that life is a love affair with a graciousness that is hopelessly in love with us. Paddy Chayefsky catches this in a remarkable passage of dialogue between Yahweh and Gideon in his play *Gideon:*

GIDEON: I thought of nothing but you the whole night. I am possessed by all the lunacy of love. If I could, I would cover you with veils, God, and keep you hidden behind the curtains in my tent. Oh! just say again you love me, God.

THE ANGEL: I do, Gideon.

GIDEON: I do not know why. I must say, I do not know why.

THE ANGEL: I hardly know why myself, but then passion is an unreasonable thing.[2]

It is terribly, terribly difficult to harmonize this world view, this interpretation of life, this pattern of meaning with our mundane, routine, frequently senseless and often tragic existence. Yet in our experiences of graciousness, we do get the hint that whatever it is that is stirring up our awe and wonder, it is overwhelming in its graciousness. We are afraid to trust our intuition that whatever or whoever is out there beyond the limits could be so gracious. Life couldn't possibly have that glorious a purpose. Could it?

Jesus came to tell us that it could and did. He knew because he knew the father better than anyone else. Christians are quite simply those who believe that Jesus was right, and that we are right when we are willing to push our intuition of graciousness to its farthest limit and even beyond. But such belief is not merely the dull assent to an abstract proposition. To believe that Jesus was right means I share in his experience of a God madly in love with me, and then live as one must who is caught up in such a love affair.

Responding to love is always difficult and awkward, but when we find that we are loved, we are happy and we rejoice. We feel like singing, dancing, celebrating, and sharing our joy with others. And we cannot help letting others in on the power of the love in which we find ourselves caught up. A young person who has discovered that he is loved is not content with sharing that love by simply describing it to others; he actually shares the love itself by trying to be as good to them as he experiences his beloved being good to him. He may make an awkward mess out of it in his naive enthusiasm, but he wants the world to know that he is loved and loves. And that is what Christianity is all about.

THEOLOGICAL NOTE

One is often asked today whether one believes in a "personal" God—a question originating in the nineteenth-century philosophizing about "life forces." The question can have two meanings that are frequently intermingled. An impersonal God can either be one that is something less than human or something more than human. Some people feel ill at ease with the thought of God as a person, because *person* has come to mean *human being,* and God is obviously more than that. Others are disturbed about using human images and language to talk about something as fundamentally indescribable as the Ultimate and the Absolute. Still others feel easier believing in an impersonal God that doesn't particularly care for us one way or another. The pertinent question is not whether God is personal or not but whether there is in the universe a plan, a purpose, a graciousness that can best be described as passionate love. Arguments about *person* evade this prior and critical issue. Obviously, human language about God is metaphorical and poetic—as is human language about a lot of things (like love) that cannot fit into precise scholarly and scientific categories. Just as obviously, it would be a mistake in language to equate our talk about God completely with our talk about our fellow humans. But a God who does not care is a God not worth taking seriously. And the Christian experience of graciousness is an experience of a Thou to whom one can respond, and who in fact seems to be waiting for a response.

NOTES

1. After each question that introduces a mystery, I include in parentheses the way the question was asked in the old catechisms. I do this to indicate that it is the same religious reality that is being discussed, however different the method of discussion.

2. Paddy Chayefsky, *Gideon*. New York: Random House, 1961, p. 67.

Chapter Two

THE MYSTERY OF
JESUS OF NAZARETH

Are there any grounds for hope?

(Who was Jesus of Nazareth?)

MOST OF OUR EFFORTS GO BADLY. THE MODEL AIRPLANE does not fly, the new home is not quite what we thought it would be, the marriage is pretty much like most other marriages, the social reform we were so committed to does not occur or does not work. The end of the war does not bring peace, the New Age never began, the job turns out to be dull, the promotion does not materialize. The children become surly, the house is always a mess, the vacation is ruined by rain, the trip to Europe is a dud. The romantic weekend is marred by sickness, the course taught by the brilliant professor becomes a bore, the anniversary celebration deteriorates into nagging and nastiness.

And even when our efforts are crowned with success they somehow still seem inadequate. Santa Claus brings everything we want and we are still not happy. We graduate and begin a new life only to discover that it is very much like the old. The girl or boy of our dreams turns out to be a disappointment after only the third date. We get the promotion, the fur coat, the summer home, the boat, the new car; and the quality of life does not change. The joys of the wedding day and night fade quickly. Our most impressive accomplishments turn sour. Our wildest expectations come true for a brief time and then become bitter. Success is almost as bad as failure. It hardly seems worth trying to succeed; failure is probable and success unsatisfying. What difference does it make? Eventually we grow old and die, so why try? Why hope? Why bother?

Yet we can no more stop hoping than we can stop breathing as long as we are still alive. Even those who are terminally ill keep on hoping. The subconscious, according to Sigmund Freud, believes in its own immortality. Our dreams, according to other researchers, assume that we are immortal. Hope is irrevocably rooted in our personalities. Perhaps it is the other side of our conviction that life has purpose. We can stop hoping only by ridding ourselves of our humanity. The only ones for whom despair is complete are those who commit suicide. They finally see nothing in which to hope at all.

Rejuvenation comes easily. A good night's sleep gives us a new lease on life. The morning sun rises and chases away the clouds, fog, and rain. Time heals the wounds of separation and loss. Illness wanes, and our bodily forces are restored. The warmth and color of spring replaces the cold drabness of winter. Friendships long dormant can begin again. Love is reborn and intimacy gets a fresh start. The failures and discouragements of the past are left behind in the full flush of our enthusiasm for a new idea, a new project, a new dream.

All our little hopes are drawn from the biggest hope of all, that maybe death does not have the final word. Every new burst of hopefulness is a gamble that it is worthwhile to hope, that even in the final moment despair is a misreading of the situation. There may seem to be little ground for hope, the gamble is a long shot; but it still seems better to live hopefully than to try to fight the immensely powerful urges toward hopefulness which continue as long as we have breath surging up from the depths of whatever is us.

But can we trust our hopefulness? Is it a trick, a deception, a mechanism the human race has developed in the course of evolutionary selection to ensure the survival of the species? Or is it the hint of an explanation, a revelation, the best single hint we have of what life is? Is the "bright golden haze on the meadow" a cheat or a sacrament?[1]

Jesus of Nazareth was the man who came to tell us that it is all right to trust our hopefulness. "Dream your most impossible dream," he tells us, in effect. "Hope your most expansive hope, fantasize your wildest fantasy, and you will have just begun. Out beyond those dreams, hopes, and fantasies, the generosity of my heavenly Father only begins. For eye has not seen nor has ear heard nor has it entered into the heart of man what the heavenly Father has prepared for those who return his love."

It is the nature of hope that it shatters our sorrows and our fears, our disappointments and our anxieties. It rushes into our personality and impatiently and irresistibly sweeps away all the obstacles that stand in its way. It tears apart our preconceptions, it blasts our imbedded gloomy explanations. It stands everything on end. "April is the cruelest month," says T. S. Eliot, because it is the month of rebirth in England. Hope has its healing effect because it enables us to see things differently, to put together the pieces of our life in a pattern we may not have tried before. Hope throws something new into the picture (or, more often, perhaps, throws a spotlight on something old, lighting it in such a way that it is almost as though we had never seen it before).

Our life can begin all over again. Love grows cold and stale, bickering replaces affection, counting up slights and injured feelings has replaced tenderness. If we let hope hold sway we can see possibilities in the other and in ourselves that were not apparent before. The angers and injuries dissolve and love is reborn. Hope has done its work.

Jesus is the man of hope. He is the Christ, the one whose words and deeds reveal the heavenly Father to us as he was never revealed before. Jesus is the "sacrament" of God, the best revelation we will ever have of what God is like. He knew the heavenly Father because he was, as he claimed, on terms of intimacy with him that no one else enjoyed. He dared to address the Father with the affectionate, almost joking title "Abba," thereby immediately setting himself off as different from all the other prophets and teachers, preachers and Saints. He knew the Father, and he came into the world with desperate urgency to tell us that we, too, could call the Father "Abba," that we, too, could live as if we were his playful children. The great dinner was ready, the wedding banquet prepared; all that was left for us was to respond to the invitation.

Like hope itself, this man of hope had a shattering impact. He turned the world upside down; and, as G. K. Chesterton said, when the world was viewed from such a remarkable perspective, it suddenly made sense. Hope, Jesus told us, was not a subject for doubt; the only things about which we could reasonably doubt were our own foolish fears, our petty suspicions, our silly anxieties.

There are powerful tensions in the life of Jesus: between gentleness and urgency, insistence on God's loving mercy and fear that time may run out; between peace and the sword; between a yoke that is sweet and light and fire on the earth; between patience with sinners and fierce anger at hypocrites; between confidence in the Father and uncertainty about how the Father will work his will.

Even the words of Jesus reveal this tension: first and last, poor and rich, called and chosen, bread and body, chalice and blood.

The tensions in the life and in the language of Jesus are the result of the power of the hope he came to reveal and to confirm. Hope shatters our old misconceptions; it enables us to start again because it impels us to see things differently. As the man of hope, Jesus had to shatter our old ways of perceiving and living so that we could see things the way they really are—filled with hopefulness—and so that we could live the way we ought to—as children of hope. Jesus is a disconcerting person because there is no other way to be a sacrament of hope.

But it is precisely the hopefulness of Jesus, and the powerful tensions he felt and generated, that have made him attractive to all who have come to know him, even those who have dismissed his hope as mad self-deception. Even today those who do not like churches or who do not accept religion are still fascinated by Jesus. He was no ordinary man, they agree; he was driven by forces that make him attractive, fascinating, and intriguing. He was probably wrong, they contend. And we might respond: What if he was right?

What indeed?

Jesus' hope was rooted in the unshakable conviction that the power of God was at work in the world. He called it the " kingdom of God, " and we sometimes call it the " reign of God." Whatever words we use, the idea is that God has a plan for the world and that plan is going forward irresistibly. Moreover, Jesus was convinced that this power of God was making a major breakthrough in his time with his appearance. This new inrushing of God's power was a turning point in the development of God's plan, an opportunity not to be missed. Now was the time to reform one's life and to begin again; now was the time to break out of the fixed, narrow, rigid routines in which humans were caught and give full and free rein to their hopefulness. Now was the time to get up and live.

Jesus was a man of his own time. Despite his special intimacy with the heavenly Father, he used the terms and the thought categories of his age. Sometimes these words and styles of thinking seem strange and foreign to us (though they should never stand in the way of our understanding him unless we insist on the mindless literalism of interpreting his words exactly the same way we would if those words were spoken to us by a man of our own time). So we must approach Jesus' words about the power of God with respect for the time and place in which he lived. We must ask what he was trying to tell us through the words he used and the style in which he thought.

There are times when he seemed to be saying that the kingdom of God was already present and other times when he was saying that it was yet to come. Sometimes the "yet to come" was very soon, and at other times it was in the unknown future. Perhaps Jesus himself was not sure. (The Scripture tells us that he grew in knowledge—learned more with the passage of time.) More than likely he was once again a man of tension: the kingdom of God was both "already" and "not yet." The power of God was already at work in the world, and now, with Jesus' coming, in a new and more definitive way; but the ultimate of that power was still to be revealed. The plan was moving forward, indeed with accelerating pace, but it was not yet fully accomplished. Our hope is already partially fulfilled, and in Jesus a promise of its ultimate fulfillment was given by a God who disclosed himself to us in and through Jesus, but the goal of that hopefulness is still obscured in the future. Life begins once again as the healing forces of hope pour into it. With Jesus, life makes a new beginning that is decisive and definitive but not yet final.

Jesus not only believed in the kingdom of God, he died for it. He was not only convinced that hope was valid, he went to his death because of that conviction. At the time of the intense experience we call the Transfiguration, Jesus saw more clearly than he had before that he would probably be taken and executed. His conviction of the power of God and the hope that flowed from that conviction had to be put to the final test of death.

Down through the ages some Christians have been so concerned about protecting the truth of the special presence of God in Jesus that they have come to deprive him of most of his humanity. Historically these people were called Monophysites (Greek for "one nature"), and in ages past were far more numerous than the Nestorians (named after the heretical bishop of Constantinople who died in 451), those Christians who virtually eliminated any special presence of God in the Jesus we know. For those people—and there were many of them among our teachers—Jesus was essentially an actor reading a script, going through a scenario. They never quite put it that way, of course, but the picture we got from them was of someone going through the motions. Jesus knew exactly what was going to happen from the beginning. He preached to his people even though he knew they would turn him down. Hence there was little reason for sorrow or a sense of failure. It was all part of the story line. He went up to Jerusalem to be executed, realizing that there would be a few bad hours but that he would rise from the dead soon. Perhaps he had the exact hour of this event already in his mind. So there was little reason for fear or anguish.

This approach to the life and death of Jesus is hard to reconcile with the Scripture stories about his sorrow over his failure and his anguish over the prospect of his own death. It makes Jesus unattractive to those who are not Christians—especially when this stage-play approach to his life is imposed as a matter of faith. But worst of all, it deprives Jesus of any common humanity with the rest of us. We all sorrow over our failures and anguish over the approach of death; we all wonder whether it has been worth the effort; we all live in terror of the cracking apart of our personality, the apparent destruction of that which is us in the ugliness of death. Everyone has a faint hope in survival. Christians firmly believe that death does not say the final word. But no matter how strong our hope in survival, we are still afraid. Survival may be plausible, reasonable, probable even, but it is not mathematically certain. If there were such certainty, there would be no need to hope.

If Jesus were certain, then he would not be one of us. We

might be impressed by his abilities as an actor, but we would have no sense of community with him. If, on the other hand, he approached Jerusalem with both confidence and fear, hope and uncertainty, about how and when he would receive his heavenly Father's validation and the confirmation of his preaching, then he was one of us. Then we share a common humanity, we can learn from him, we can go up to Jerusalem with him.

The Christians who would turn Jesus into an actor are afraid that one cannot combine confidence and fear, hope and uncertainty, anguish and expectation, terror and faith. The rest of us do it every day, of course, but somehow it does not seem right for Jesus to have suffered it. So, for these Christians, Jesus goes up to Jerusalem on one path unanxious and untroubled; and we take another path frightened and hopeful. Such Christians should read the Scripture more closely. If Jesus were not going up to Jerusalem with us, there would have been no point in going at all.

So Jesus went to his death with fear and anguish but with hope and confidence also. He knew that the power of God would guarantee that his death would not be in vain; he knew that death would have no final victory over him; he knew that the power of God would sweep away the temporary triumph of death. But he also knew he had to die.

Jesus claimed a special intimacy with the Father. Christians believe that God revealed himself to us in a special way through Jesus; hence his hope was necessarily special. Indeed the whole point of Jesus' life was that he disclosed to us a vision of hope based on his intimacy with God, in which we would not dare believe and to which we would not dare commit ourselves (though we would have perhaps occasionally glimpsed its possibility) were it not for Jesus.

So Jesus went to his death with a special hope. He knew the heavenly Father would vindicate him against his enemies and against the final enemy, death. But the specialness of his hope came from its depth, its breadth, its intensity; it came from the unique nature of the union between Jesus and the heavenly Father. However, the specialness did not consist of a knowledge about the specificity of the details of time, manner, and mode of his vindication. Jesus knew he would win; he did not know how. Such is the anguish of all human life—no matter how hopeful.

Jesus was supremely confident of the triumph of God's plan and of his own victory as the revelation of that plan. God's kingdom would succeed as certainly as does the seed become the tree, as does the tiny grain grow into the harvest. Nothing could stand in its way. Thus one does all one can to seize this pearl of great price, this buried treasure. One plots and schemes, as did the unjust steward, so as not to lose it. One has the wedding garment and is ready to take advantage of every possibility that is offered. One eagerly responds to the invitation before the doors of the banquet hall are closed. In confidence of the success in gaining God's kingdom, one can stop by the wayside to assist an injured enemy. In other words, one lives a life of courage, vigor, confidence, commitment, and generosity. One never stops trying, never gives up, never sinks into a rut, never turns back, never refuses an opportunity to help, never rejects the possibility of reconciliation, never thinks that it is too late to begin again. For the follower of Jesus who hopes in the kingdom of God, tomorrow is not merely the first day of the rest of his life; tomorrow will also be different even when today is the last of his life.

From what we know of Jesus it seems safe to assume that he and his followers sang psalms as they went up to Jerusalem. So we must join them on that final journey on which we are all embarked. We must go up to our own Jerusalem with fear and anguish but also with confidence and hope, with joy in our hearts and a song on our lips. There is no other way to live.

THEOLOGICAL NOTES

1. The followers of Jesus in their Easter experience of him finally saw clearly that which had seemed so obscure during his ministry. He was human like us but he was also something more than human. God was present in him in a unique and special way. Jesus claimed this special intimacy, and the resurrection experience validated that claim. Since Easter, Christians have tried to cope with the paradox of "human like us" and "something more than human." It is a paradox ignored by the mindless question, "Do you believe in the divinity of Jesus?" Of course, any follower of Jesus believes the divinity to be present in Jesus, but that is no great feat of faith; God is present in all of us. What is at issue is the special presence of God in Jesus in a unique way that still leaves him a person like us. The Christian must believe in both at the same time; the data of the Scripture and the teaching of Christian tradition leave him no choice. The theological explanation of this paradox (called the Incarnation) has preoccupied Christians almost since the beginning with heat rather than light being generated on many occasions. Many different formulations of the paradox have been attempted in the past—none of them completely satisfactory. Christian faith is not held to particular philosophical formulations, and theologians are struggling today to restate the Incarnation in ways that will convey the truth of "human like us" and "something more than human," and in terms that will mean to modern humans what the Greek philosophical terms used to mean to those who were alive in the days of the early councils.

Such a task of reformulation is both delicate and necessary. No useful purpose is served by charging heresy against those who, in sincerity and good faith, try to restate the paradox in terms that will be meaningful for those whose religious needs are not served by the rote repetition of ancient formulas deprived of all the tension and anguish that went into their construction. The dangers in reformulation today seem to be more Nestorian (denying the "something more than human") than Monophysitic (denying the "human like us"). If one rejects the special and unique intimacy between God and Jesus, then one simply is no longer part of that tradition that traces itself back to the Easter experience. However, most serious Catholic theologians are not so simplistic in their approach. Whatever the results of their efforts, however, we are still going to have to believe in someone who is "human like us" and still "something more than human."

2. Did Jesus expect the imminent end of the world? This question has become especially important because some early twentieth-century writers—most notably, the famous Albert Schweitzer —insisted that Jesus was nothing more than an eschatological teacher preparing his followers for an end of the world that he thought was close at hand. This idea continues to exist in the popular imagination even though most scholars now reject it in its most simple form. It is clear that there was widespread expectation of the imminent end in the religious thinking (pagan as well as Jewish) during the time of Jesus. It is also quite clear that many of the followers of Jesus, men of their own era that they were, gave an apocalyptic (end of the world) coloration to the way they handed down the teaching of Jesus. They were gravely disappointed when the world survived the destruction of Jerusalem. The scripture evidence for what Jesus thought is ambiguous. He spoke of both the kingdom already present in himself and of the kingdom yet to come. He resisted attempts to get him to define the "when" of the "yet to come." His sense of urgency was based more on the enormous opportunity the kingdom offered than on any sense of the temporal limitations to the possibility of response—other than those imposed by the shortness of human life.

Still it is possible that he may have been enough of a man of his own time to have anticipated with his human knowledge a fulfillment of God's plan in the relatively near future. The ambiguity of the Scriptures results from the fact that we cannot be sure how much the followers of Jesus were reading their own culturally induced apocalyptic expectations into what Jesus actually said. The best scholarly investigations seem to suggest that apocalyptic expectations were at an absolute minimum in the preaching of Jesus himself—thus bringing us to almost the exact opposite position to that taken by Schweitzer.

Note

1. In its original sense the word *sacrament* meant "something to reveal a great secret, a great mystery."

Chapter Three

THE MYSTERY OF THE SPIRIT

Is it safe to trust?

(Is the Holy Spirit God?)

W<small>E LIVE TRAPPED IN FEAR. WE ARE AFRAID OF LOSING OUR</small> jobs, of being ridiculed by our friends, that people will talk, that we will be failures, that our spouses may be unfaithful, that we may get cancer. We fear that we are not raising our children properly, that the neighborhood will deteriorate, that we may be mugged, that the airplane may crash. We may be out of fashion or, even worse, old-fashioned.

On a more cosmic level we fear thermonuclear war, too much ozone in the lower air and not enough in the upper air. We are afraid of earthquakes, depression, recession, inflation, and world famine. The Ice Age may return, our country may turn into a desert, foreign nations may overtake us, the world may come to an end.

We may even die. Indeed, we will die. So we are afraid of sickness, disease, hospitals, and doctors. Above all, and quite reasonably so, we are afraid to die. And worse than physical dissolution at the end are those daily deaths of self and the fear of being tricked, chumped, taken advantage of, deceived, made a fool of, and put down. They may laugh at us, and then we would die of shame.

And all the other fears are linked to that one. Shame is the fear of being cut off, seen through, destroyed, put out of existence. When we are ashamed, we die a bit; and no one wants to die even a little bit.

So we build up massive walls of protection around our bodies and spirits. We will protect ourselves so that we need never feel shame. We will have so many defenses that we don't need to think about death. We amass material goods, power, pleasure, and prestige as guarantees against death. They do not provide us with permanent security, of course, but for at least a time they do offer the illusion of security.

We invent defense mechanisms to keep others at bay. We are silent and reserved so that they will think us strong. We must always have our way. And, so that they will think we are dominant, we can never admit that we are wrong (much less apologize). We often become nasty, vindictive, tyrannical, and unreasonable so that they will be afraid of us. Or, so that they will take pity on us, we become weak, pathetic, dependent, and incapable of coping. We turn to neuroses, to compulsions and obsessions, to erratic and unpredictable behavior, to paralyzing fears, even to physical symptoms of illness in order to focus attention away from who and what we truly are. We take up drink or drugs or excessive eating or compulsive work or sex to kill the pain of our fears. We kill ourselves slowly in order to protect ourselves from the sudden death by shame of being seen for what we really are. We never stop running.

So we live our tight, narrow, rigid, frightened, inflexible, dull lives. Any other way of living would involve our taking intolerable risks. We become cautious, careful, somber, grim, and conservative. It is a very dangerous pilgrimage that we are on, and there are many dragons and demons lurking in the bushes alongside the road. If we are not wary we will be in deep trouble.

Yet there are interludes when all of this fear seems foolish, when we see dimly that it is possible to live differently. These times seem to come particularly at the turning points of our lives—the dawn of reflective self-awareness in adolescence, the beginning of serious thought a few years later, our first serious love, marriage, having a child, crossing the crucial markers of thirty, when we are no longer young; at forty, when we begin to get old, and then in the last years, when we can look back at what our life has been. At each of these times we may briefly glimpse other options available to us. We sense that we are free to choose. We can continue down the path of dull, bland, fearful mediocrity, or strike out bravely and boldly, becoming someone very different yet remaining our own true self.

It is almost as though we were on one bank of a river and there was someone else on the other side calling to us. He is beckoning to us and we seem to hear the words that Jesus said to Lazarus when he brought him out of the tomb: "Come forth."

This call to come forth, to leave foolish fears behind, to take risks, to trust, to begin to live, comes to us urgently from other human beings. We are made with the capacity to challenge and to be challenged by others, to be stirred up, "turned on." The attractiveness of other humans, as well as their tenderness, opens up to us the possibility of intimacy with them. We quickly learn that intimacy can only succeed if one is willing to give death to shame and let the other one see us as we really are, taking the risk that he might laugh at us, ridicule us, break our heart. Intimacy can be achieved only if we are willing to be defenseless, vulnerable; it can survive only if we are willing to give to the other such untrammeled power over us that he can break our heart. In an intimate relationship we must remain vulnerable; we must knock down defenses every day of our lives.

Marriage is the intimate relationship par excellence. It is in marriage that most humans receive the principal challenge to come forth. It is through marital intimacy that we hear the voice from across the river, assuring us that there is nothing to fear, that it is safe to trust. The sheer power of physical passion and pleasure draws the bodies of man and woman together; they are driven to reveal themselves physically to one another, and in that revelation they discover the possibility of something even greater —though the possibility may be only dimly and fleetingly perceived. But the very intimacy of their bodies creates interpersonal tensions and frictions. Their life together combines the joy of physical union and the friendship of shared experience with the constant aggravation of the conflicts involved in a common life. The man and woman either open themselves up to one another, slowly and laboriously constructing a life together, or they pull back into themselves and settle for a marriage that is "like every other marriage," in which fear, defensiveness, shame, stored up hurts, and petty punishments alternate with bursts of passion—ever more infrequent—that seem to have increasingly less meaning.

Still, on occasion, they may faintly hear the voice telling them that it need not be this way, that it is still possible to begin anew, to start all over again.

Jesus came to tell us that the voice we hear calling to us is inviting us to the wedding feast; it is the Spirit of God, the Spirit who hovered over the waters when God called forth life.

> Play music in Yahweh's honor, you devout,
> remember his holiness, and praise him.
> His anger lasts a moment, his favor a lifetime;
> in the evening, a spell of tears, in the morning, shouts of joy.
>
> "Hear, Yahweh, take pity on me;
> Yahweh, help me!"
> You have turned my mourning into dancing,
> you have stripped off my sackcloth and wrapped me in
>   gladness;

and now my heart, silent no longer, will play you music;
Yahweh, my God, I will praise you forever
(Ps 30: 4,5; 10–12).

Friedrich Nietzsche, the somber German philosopher, told us that the only God worth believing in is a dancing God. He was right; and the Holy Spirit is the Lord of the Dance.

Jesus told his apostles that they need not be afraid when he left them to return to the Father, because the Spirit would come to them. The Spirit is light, fire, and wind. The Spirit's light is truth, the Spirit's fire is passionate commitment, the Spirit's wind is enthusiasm. The great wind and the tongues of flame at Pentecost showed the Spirit "turning on" the apostles, filling them with a confidence and an enthusiasm that sent them out to convert the world.

The Spirit is the paraclete, the helper, the advocate, the comforter. The Spirit calls us forth with his dazzling fire and his howling wind; but he also encourages us and reassures us when we are discouraged and frightened. The Spirit calls us forth out of our narrow fears and our timid anxieties by stirring us up, by attracting us, and then by reassuring us when the fears and timidities reappear. And thus it is with any lover whose beloved is fearful and hesitant.

The Father is the God who creates, the Son is the God who speaks, the Spirit is the God who calls. The mystery of the Holy Spirit does not tell us that life is completely safe. It does not tell us that despite all evidence to the contrary we can trust everyone and take every risk. It does not assure us that we will not get hurt. It does not hide from us the evil of death. It does not claim to protect us from all the pain that vulnerability entails. The mystery of the Holy Spirit merely tells us that there are grounds for trust, that it is all right to take risks, and that being vulnerable to others is a better way to live.

We will get hurt sometimes. We will fail often, we will be ridiculed frequently, we will be rejected occasionally, and we will be shamed at least once in a while; but we will only die once. It is not safe over on the other side of the river; on the contrary it is more dangerous. But it is a much better place to be, and whichever side we choose, death will find us.

The mystery of the Holy Spirit, then, reveals to us that the pains, the failures, the rejections, the ridicule, the shame we risk in the open life are not permanent. They are costs we must pay in the search for satisfaction, growth, and love. They are costs that are worth it because through them we learn how to love. And no matter how great the pain, the Holy Spirit, the healer, will bind up our wounds, soothe our hurts, heal our injuries, erase our shame, and encourage us to try again.

Life is not easy, but the doctrine of the Holy Spirit tells us that the full life is possible. Growth is painful, but the doctrine of the Holy Spirit tells us that we can still grow. The intimate vulnerability that is required for love is terrifying, but the mystery of the Holy Spirit tells us that with all the agonies and sorrows abroad in the world it is a place where it is safe enough to love. The Holy Spirit guarantees it.

But the Spirit does not remake us. The apostles on Pentecost were not turned into men they never were before. Rather they became themselves for the first time. The Spirit called out of them that which was most creative, most courageous, most generous, most fully and completely human; and he does that to us, too. He broke through the barriers of the apostle's petty ambitions, their blind materialism, their cowardly fears; and he can do that for us, too. The Spirit did not transform Peter and James and John and the rest into totally new human beings. He liberated that which was best in each of them. He did not attempt to create a new kind of man. He spoke to those depths of the personality of each apostle who had already heard his call but feared to respond. Saint Paul tells us that the Spirit speaks to our spirit. The God who calls speaks to that spark of divinity that is in each one of us. The God without speaks to the hunger for God within. God's Spirit touches that finest, sharpest point in our personality, the very core of our identity, which tells us that we can be far more than we are. With the unerring instinct of a skillful lover, the Spirit knows exactly how to turn us on; he knows our weak link, which is in fact our greatest strength. He calls us from across the river with telling impact, because he knows that beneath our terrors and rigidities and hesitations, we want to respond.

We are free not to go. We can hear the invitation to the dance with the Spirit and turn it down. We know that part of us wants to let the Spirit blow us whither he wills, but another part of us is afraid to take the chance. What would happen? What would people say? Isn't it much safer to cool it, to run no risks, to take no chances? We have only one life, and we ought to live it cautiously. It is better to rust out than to burn out, better to oxidize slowly rather than explode in a great burst of flame.

Start with my toes,
you old Ghost
Spirit the soles of my shoes
and teach me a Pentecostal
Boogaloo
Sprain my ankles with dancing
Sandal around my feet,
to roam with me in the rain
and feel at home in my footprints.

Oh! look at me spinning,
Sprinkling, tonguing teaching
Winsoming wondrous steps
lift me, how!?
We'd better quit now,

too all dizzy down giggly
Stop—you're tickling
(my funnybone's fickle for you)
Stop—I'll drop. I'm dying,
I'm flying with your winding my feet and
legs and waist
Lassoed

Stop chasing fool—I'm racing from you
Don't catch me
Do!
I'll drown!
Oh, drown me—most
For I love you so,
You old Ghost!

Poem for Pentecost
Nancy McCready

The God who creates is the principle of unity in the universe; the God who calls is the principle of variety and diversity. The more special each one of us becomes when we respond to that which is most authentically us, the more different we become from others. And as more human beings respond to the Spirit that speaks to that which is most creative in themselves, the greater the variety and heterogeneity in the world. The spirit of this world tells us not to be different, to stay in line, to go along, to avoid the deadly sanctions which envy can impose, to flee from the risks of self-revelation and the shame of having that which is most secret in us seen by all. The spirit of this world wants to keep the world a neat, orderly, gray, dull place.

The Holy Spirit, the Spirit of and beyond this world, wants the human world to abound with the same wild profligate diversity which can be seen in the world of rocks, the world of plants, the world of animals. Only among humankind is it possible to resist the impulse of the variety-crazed Spirit. Bluebirds do not decide to be blue, the Grand Canyon cannot give up its many hues, the petunia cannot refuse to blossom, the fish darting among the corals cannot decide that its beauty is irrelevant. Only we humans can say no to the Spirit as he wheels and deals through the universe, twirling and whirling, dancing and leaping, spinning and jumping, shooting forth sparks of this divine creativity wherever he goes. We are the only ones who can say: "Thanks, Holy Spirit, but no thanks."

We can turn in on ourselves, pile up our earthly possessions, amass power and prestige, lead narrow, rigid, futile, desperate lives. We can become so atrophied that we don't hear the call from across the river and are unable to disregard those faint whispers and echoes that may intrude.

God's Spirit, then, is a spirit of creativity, variety, and enthusiasm. He is not, however, a spirit of mindless irrationality. If he speaks to that which is best in us, he certainly speaks to our minds as well as to our emotions. Spontaneity and creativity are not the same thing as undisciplined frenzy. The Spirit liberates the authentic self, not the unrestrained libidinal *id*. The dance of the Spirit is not the dance of drunken revelers. False spirits, as well as the Holy Spirit, are abroad in the world. The voices we hear in the night may be voices of evil, irresponsibility, and destruction. The most destructive of undisciplined human enthusiasms both to the individual person and to the social order are those that confidently but naively claim to be inspired by the Holy Spirit, when in fact they are in the possession of the spirits of madness, of this world, and of all those little hurts, angers, and resentments that have been turned in on the self for so long.

So we must listen carefully to make sure that it is God's Spirit who inspires us to make a decisive change in our life, to begin anew, to start all over again, to break with the past, to commit ourselves enthusiastically to a new vision. There is always a risk in change, and the risk becomes even greater when we realize that we may be deceiving ourselves about what is motivating our change. Instead of stripping away the barriers and defenses so that we can become truly ourselves, it may be that we have simply found a new means of keeping ourselves hidden from others. Now we can cope with the intimate stranger who threatens us so terribly by attacking him in the name of authenticity and enthusiasm, in the name of the Spirit. We aggressively try to strip away the defenses of others and pretend we are being open ourselves.

How can we tell whether it is God's Spirit or the spirit of this world who is speaking to us? If it is God's Spirit there is no nervousness; no frantic, fierce, anxious tensions; no desperate need to convince or to convert others; no compulsion to force others to share in our joy. God's Spirit brings peace, patience, kindness, tolerance, generosity, gentleness, tenderness, perseverance, serenity, openness, and respect for the freedom of others. If our new beginning, our rebirth, our new enthusiasm, and our sudden discovery of self are not marked by those characteristics, then they are the work of a false spirit, a spirit of hatred, punishment, and self-deception.

Most human activities are the result of complex, intricate motivations. It is hard to tell whether it is the Holy Spirit who is blowing us along with new energy and vigor or a howling demon of fear and anxiety, masquerading as a good spirit. It often seems that both spirits are at work at the same time. We must listen carefully. If it turns out that we are not more loving to those who are closest to us, which often means that they do not perceive us as more loving, then the Holy Spirit is losing the contest.

Many Christians have come to believe that the Christian life consists of discreet, cautious, and sober respectability. They are offended by the idea of a spirit of variety, a lord of the dance. Surely there are times in human life when discretion, caution, sobriety, and respectability are very much in order. The indisputable Christians, the apostles and the saints, could be discreet and cautious when the occasion called for it, but such behavior was not the hallmark of their lives. On the contrary, they were so outgoing, so open, so vulnerable to others, so generous, so creative, so ready to run risks, so eager to trust in the fundamental goodness of their lives that they often seemed to their friends and neighbors to be just a little bit mad.

You will remember that that is what the relatives of Jesus and the crowds who attended to the enthusiasm of the apostles on Pentecost thought. What a shame that grown men should be drunk so early in the morning!

We all know such people, men and women of sensitive, well-disciplined enthusiasm who are a joy to be with, who challenge and attract us while they are comforting and reassuring us at the same time. They may seem a little bizarre at times, and we both envy and hate them for their freedom and creativity. (If we could, we, too, might well try to crucify him.) Still we admire them. A world composed of such men and women would be much less predictable and well-ordered and respectable than the one in which we now live. By our inflexible standards, it might even seem a bit crazy; but it would be a more joyous and happy place.

That's what God's Spirit has in mind.

THEOLOGICAL NOTE

The doctrine of the Holy Trinity was not revealed to us to test our faith or to provide an abstruse puzzle for metaphysically inclined theologians. It was revealed to tell us something about God, and hence something about the purpose and meaning of human life. Briefly, the doctrine of the Trinity means that while God is one, he is not solitary. God is rational, God is interactive, God is a community, God is interpersonal love. The God who creates, the God who speaks, and the God who calls have been involved in an eternal love affair with one another and are now inviting us to join their dance of loving joy and joyous love. If the invitation is frightening, the reason is that we are being asked to join very fast company. But we are free to bring our friends.

Liturgical Note

Dancing is making a comeback in Christian liturgy today. Rightfully so, as it was part of the liturgy in days gone by. In the early centuries, Christians danced at martyrs' tombs or in churches in their honor on the vigil of the martyr's feast. In medieval France there were dances in the churches on Christmas and Easter that involved the bishops and the priests. In Spain, in the last century, dances in church marked the Feasts of the Immaculate Conception and Corpus Christi. Even today in Seville young boys in peasant garb dance a pavane in the cathedral in the presence of the blessed sacrament exposed on the altar, and accompany their dance with castanets. The medieval carol "My Dancing Day" echoes this Christian insight about a dancing God.

> *Tomorrow shall be my dancing day,*
> *I would my true love did so chance*
> *To see the legend of my play,*
> *To call my true love to my dance.*
>
> *Sing, oh! my love, oh! my love, my love, my love,*
> *This have I done for my true love.*
>
> *Then was I born of a Virgin pure,*
> *Of her, I took fleshy substance;*
> *Thus was I born of a Virgin pure,*

To call my true love to my dance.
Sing, oh! my love, oh! my love, my love, my love,
This have I done for my true love.
Then on the cross hanged I was,
Where a spear to my heart did glance;
There issued forth water and blood
To call my true love to my dance.

Sing, oh! my love, oh! my love, my love, my love,
Then down to Hell I took my way
For my true love's deliverance,
And rose again on the third day
Up to my true love and the dance

Sing, oh! etc.

Then up to Heaven I did ascend,
Where now I dwell is sure substance,
On the right hand of God, that man
May come unto the general dance.

Sing, oh! etc.

(Quoted in William Sandys, *Christmas Carols, Ancient and Modern*, London: Richard Beckley, 1833.)

The same theme has been echoed more recently in the song, "Lord of the Dance," sung to the Shaker hymn "Simple Gifts."

I danced in the morning when the world was begun,
And I danced in the moon and stars and the sun,
And I came down from heaven and I danced on the earth;
At Bethlehem I had my birth.

(Refrain) Dance then wherever you may be;
I am the Lord of the Dance, said he,
And I'll lead you all, wherever you may be,
And I'll lead you all in the dance, said he.

I danced for the scribe and the Pharisee,
but they wouldn't dance, and they wouldn't follow me;

I danced for the fishermen, for James and John;
They came with me and the dance went on.
(Refrain)

I danced on the Sabbath and I cured the lame;
The holy people said it was a shame.
They whipped and they stripped and they hung me high,
And left me there on a cross to die.
(Refrain)

I danced on a Friday when the sky turned black;
It's hard to dance with the devil on your back.
They buried my body and they thought I'd gone;
But I am the dance and I still go on.
(Refrain)

They cut me down and I leapt up high;
I am the life that'll never, never die;
I'll live in you if you'll live in me:
I am the Lord of the Dance, said he:
(Refrain)

("Lord of the Dance" American Shaker Melody. Arr. by
Sydney Carter [b. 1915]. Copyright © 1963 by Galliard Ltd. All
Rights Reserved. Used by permission.)

Chapter Four

THE MYSTERY OF THE CROSS
AND RESURRECTION

Why is there evil in the world?

(Why did Jesus Christ die on the cross?)

T HERE IS EVIL IN THE WORLD. EARTHQUAKES WIPE OUT hundreds of thousands of lives, over 20 million people died in the Spanish influenza plague of 1918, one-third of Europe succumbed to the Black Death. Children are starving to death in South Asia. Poverty, ignorance, and malnutrition afflict the majority of the human race. Scores die in rush-hour commuter train accidents. Children are brutalized by their parents. Teenagers start off in a bus on a carefree picnic and end up going to their deaths. A young woman is killed by robbers on her honeymoon. Six million Jews are exterminated in concentration camps. Twenty million Vietnamese are killed in a "war of liberation." Pictures of refugees fleeing from some terror fill our television screens several times a month. The terrorist attacks of September 11, 2001, are emblazoned into our brains and our very being. The line between being at peace and being at war grows finer every day.

Hurricanes wipe out towns and villages. Urban slums become jungles of crime and vice. The environment is being thoughtlessly polluted. Whole species of birds, animals, and fish are heedlessly destroyed. Natural resources are wasted without reason. Prejudice, bigotry, arrogance, and fear keep many people in subjection. Anger, hatred, and the desire for revenge lead the oppressed to strike out against the oppressors even though those who are destroyed are frequently innocent children, harmless old people, and ordinary citizens who have nothing to do with oppression.

Leaders are gunned down in the streets, prisoners are tortured. Elementary freedoms and liberties are destroyed. Indigenous cultures are uprooted in the name of a progress that turns out to be worse than what it replaced. Schools turn into custodial institutions for the children of the poor. The streets of the cities become unsafe. Violence is as American as cherry pie.

Droughts and floods combine to destroy crops, forcing up the price of food and causing something dangerously close to a world food shortage. Unemployment and inflation threaten to tear the world economy apart. The black lung disease kills coal miners. Needless industrial accidents kill or maim tens of thousands every year. Contaminated water and poisoned air lead to an increase in cancer. "Saturday night specials" create an ever-increasing murder rate. Highway accidents, mostly caused by drunken drivers, produce more deaths each year than the dubious foreign wars that snuff out young lives at their very beginning. Drug addiction turns young people into hardened criminals, and alcoholism torments the families of millions.

The great hopes of historic events like the Vatican Council are blighted by subsequent failures. We are unjustly punished by our parents, rejected by our friends, hated by our enemies, downgraded by our rivals, weakened by the poison of envy, betrayed by those we trusted, deeply wounded by those we love.

But the question is not why does a baby die in his crib, a

young man in a napalm raid, a young woman in a gas chamber, a middle-aged man of a heart attack, a mother of cancer, a child because of the carelessness of a hit-and-run driver. All of us are under the sentence of death; some simply have it executed earlier and more unjustly than others. But it is unjust that we have to die. We are the only bodily creatures made with sufficient self-consciousness to know that we are going to die and to be sorry for it. We want with all the force that we can command to escape the sentence of death.

Yet we shall die, and our attempts to avoid it succeed only in postponing the inevitable. It is a bitter cruelty to be created with a hunger for immortality and then be denied sustenance. Maybe it would have been better had we never existed.

But we also experience good. The crops do produce food for tables. The blue sky hangs like a velvet awning above our heads. The heat wave breaks. Winter passes away and the snow and ice are replaced by the flowers of spring. The species does make slow, tortuous progress against oppression, misery, injustice, and hatred. Most diseases are curable, plagues are controlled, polio is virtually eliminated, despots are overthrown, some reforms work. Our children grow up and sometimes become our friends; conflicts do end in reconciliation; marriages get patched up; love does survive misunderstanding, thoughtlessness, and indifference. Wars end, old enemies become friends, we forgive others and are forgiven by them.

So there is a struggle between good and evil going on in the world. It goes on in the physical cosmos, in the world community, in human society, within our own personality. Evil seems much the stronger of the two, but it has not yet carried the day. Good is remarkably resilient. It always seems endangered, threatened, close to rout, yet it manages to survive and even to win victories. The outcome of the battle between good and evil remains in doubt, but evil, for all its ugly power, has yet to succeed in driving good from the earth and from the human condition. Good survives, sometimes just barely, but it survives nevertheless.

Yet does not evil win the final battle against the particular good that is in us? Is not all our struggle for growth, for trust, for love, no matter how generously waged or how successfully accomplished, finally cancelled out in the nothingness of death? Perhaps slowly, perhaps quickly, perhaps easily, perhaps with excruciating pain, we will die. Our friends will offer sympathy at the wake, prayers will be mumbled over us, our cold body will be put into colder ground, and dirt will be heaped on top of us. In a little while only a few people will remember us, and then we will be completely forgotten, as they too follow us to the grave. What purpose was served by our love?

But we are not sure. The sun sets only to rise again, nature dies in the autumn only to revive in the spring, hatred sometimes leads to reconciliation, love grows through conflict that is resolved; animals and plants die, but their substance is absorbed by other living creatures. Good survives by turning the apparent victory of evil into a victory of its own. "Birth and Death [are] inseparable on earth;/For they are twain yet one, and Death is Birth," says the poet Francis Thompson.

We experience death and rebirth often in our own lives. We pass the test, we overcome the fear, we break through the barriers of shame and timidity, we make progress against our inflexibility and defensiveness, we learn from our mistakes. In fact, we discover with time and experience that progress and growth in the human condition—whether it be personal or social—is always accomplished through a series of deaths and rebirths. In the psychotherapeutic experience in particular, we learn that we can only rise to the new human—the more free, more open, more confident, more authentic self—by dying to the old person, that narrow, anxious, fearful, defense-ridden self. We become more human and society becomes more just only through death and resurrection.

Such insight does not solve the problem of evil, because in the nature of things it is not a problem to be solved. To set up evil as a problem that, if solved, will legitimate the existence of God is both to misunderstand the question and to load the dice against any but the agnostic answer. Agnosticism is conceded in the phrasing of the question. Even if the problem of evil is not solved (and it cannot be), the "problem" of good remains. How account for evil if there is a God? But how account for good if there is not?

So the real problem is the war in heaven (and everywhere else, of course) between good and evil. Whoever wishes to look calmly and coolly (if such be possible) at the full dilemma must face the existence of good and evil or, more precisely and less philosophically, the mystery of life and death. What is ultimately baffling is not death but life. The most pointed and most poignant question is not why we die, but why we live at all.

The Christ experience does not reveal to us any rational, metaphysical solution to the problem of evil. It does not explain why there is evil in the world; it surely does not pretend that there is no evil or that it can be glossed over easily. The Christ event reveals to us merely that evil is not ultimate and good is; death does not have the final word, life does. And hence we live, not dominated by the fear of death but filled with the expectation of life. This is revealed to us through the mystery of the cross and resurrection of Jesus.

Like all humans, Jesus was deeply involved in the struggle between good and evil, between life and death. He preached life, forgiveness, joy, love, the Good News. He was misunderstood, envied, harassed, hounded, hated. His friends expected a temporal kingdom despite clear indications that the kingdom of God was not of this world. He was a healing presence, yet the crowds expected spectacular signs and wonders that he would not give them. He taught the fulfillment of the promise Yahweh made to the Hebrews, yet the leaders of the people feared and envied him.

He came to bring life, indeed "life more abundant," yet he spent the last year of his life "on the run" to escape those who would kill him. Finally, he bravely went up to Jerusalem to confront those who wanted to destroy him, won all the points in direct argument, was betrayed by a friend, treacherously arrested in the dark of night, deserted by his friends, convicted on trumped-up charges, tortured and beaten, and then executed by a cruel death reserved for rebels and slaves.

If this is what God does to his friends, who needs him? If this is what he permits to happen to one who was on terms of special intimacy with him, who claimed to be his son in a unique way, why would we trust God at all? Who wants to be the son of a father like that?

But, as happens so often, evil did not have the final word. The defeat of life somehow got turned into victory. Death did not have final dominion over Jesus. He lived and still lives. Despite the fact that it was the last thing they expected or wanted, the friends of Jesus did encounter him once again as very much alive; they encountered him repeatedly in circumstances under which their initial doubts, suspicions, hesitations, and disbelief could not survive. The Lord was truly risen. They could not explain (and neither can we) exactly how it happened, but it did happen; and they had to rush forth to tell the Good News to all the world, to cast his fire on the earth. The fire is still being cast, though in some times and in some places it has not come very close to the vigor and enthusiasm of those who encountered Jesus in the Easter experience.

The real question is not so much whether we believe that Jesus rose from the dead (though one cannot be a Christian if one does not believe. What else is the faith all about?) but whether we believe that we too shall rise. The resurrection of Jesus is a "sacrament," a dazzling burst of illumination that brings light to the darkness in which we live. It does not solve the problem of evil; rather it tells us that in the end the greatest evil of all will lose.

Life conquers death. My life will conquer my death. All of our lives will conquer all of our deaths. The hints we have that death is not final, the suspicions we experience that the resurrection experiences of our ordinary life are revelatory, the ineradicable hunch from which we cannot escape that life is stronger than death—these are confirmed, validated, ratified, and reinforced by the resurrection of Jesus—it is not outside the realm of rational possibility that somehow, some way, a single man should have managed to survive death. If that were all the faith Christianity required, one could stretch a point and make the commitment to Christianity with some feeling of rationality and common sense. Such a rational commitment would require little further in the way of expectation of the marvelous, the unexpected, the wonderful, the surprising. Neither would it demand of us an involvement like that of Jesus in the bitter struggle between good and evil that rages in the world.

But that is not what Christianity is. We are required to believe that all men will live just as Jesus did; and we are required to live just as Jesus did, committing ourselves fully and completely to the battle against evil even when we know it will win at least one cruel, vicious, arbitrary victory over us when it destroys us in death. We battle on, because we also know that even the one inevitable victory will be reversed. This is a profoundly optimistic belief. It affronts common sense. How can we believe something that sounds too good to be true?

The demand of the mystery of the cross and resurrection also terrifies us. Surely it is not necessary to live the way Jesus did, to serve other humans so completely and totally, to heal them so lovingly, to tolerate them so patiently, to pursue them so generously. Surely it is not necessary to face death so bravely and confidently. Surely it is not necessary to defy evil so contemptuously.

But the challenge of the "sacrament" of the cross and resurrection also attracts us, fascinates us, and tempts us. It resonates with our own best hopes, our own deepest inklings, our own most intractable convictions. It appeals to our best dreams— dreams we have whether we want them or not. It confirms our most optimistic suspicions, it reinforces our brightest expectations.

It probably is too good to be true. But still, what if it is?

If it is true, we will certainly have to change our lives. Those who expect to rise like Jesus will have to live and die like him. And such a life and death, such a reenactment in one person of the cosmic war between good and evil is a terrifying alternative to our present dull, complacent, mediocre life. But we all secretly suspect, in our most reflective moments and with our wisest insights, that such may be the only really human way to live after all.

The cross and the resurrection of Jesus tell us that what we had secretly hoped for, and secretly feared because of its demands, is indeed too good to be true, but is true nevertheless. Its challenge follows from every one of the great mysteries: What are you going to do about it?

The follower of Jesus does not deny evil or attempt to minimize its power. He believes in the cross of Jesus, and hence must face honestly and bluntly the ugliness and the strength of the evil that could do so terrible a thing to so good a man. But he does not despair over evil and give in to it. He believes in the resurrection of Jesus and knows that evil is not the finality. He does not retreat into the desert to escape the incurable evil of the world, because he believes in both cross and resurrection and because he knows that, like Jesus, he must dedicate himself to the eradication of evil from the earth. He must heal, console, teach, encourage, admonish, assist even if death will be the ultimate reward of his goodness.

So wherever we find the sick, the suffering, the ignorant, the hungry, the oppressed, the frightened, the lonely, the homeless, we will also find the followers of Jesus. They are there because the Lord himself has told us that it is in such places we will find him.

The best hint of an explanation of the mystery of good and evil to be found in the cross and resurrection of Jesus is that through suffering he came alive. The cross not only preceded the resurrection, in some deep way that we cannot fully understand but that seems to resonate well with our own experiences, it caused the resurrection. By dying with such courage and faith, Jesus, through the help of the heavenly Father, won resurrection. Life not only triumphs over death but somehow flows out of it. Death is not merely a prelude to life in the new man but also a cause; this is a commonplace of psychological growth inside or outside the therapeutic process. We can only rise if we are willing to go through death, not just as antecedent in time but also as it is precisely the liberation from fear of death that causes resurrection.

This profound psychological insight should not be turned into a law of physical science, but humanly we know that we begin to live free lives when we stop worrying about death. Death may then not be merely the end of life, it also may be its crowning moment; for in death all the energies and commitments of a life are focused into a single climactic moment. We will, of course, be afraid (as Jesus was in the Garden of Olives), but if we have lived as free people we will die as free people, and the fear will not wipe out the dignity and the grace of our humanity. In the moment of death we will feel the first inkling of resurrection; we have already beaten death.

And when the good and gentle Jesus reaches out to touch our hand as he touched the hand of the son of the widow of Naim, and as he says to us as he did to Lazarus, "Come forth," there is just the possibility that we may sit up, look around in surprise, and say, "Is this it? Why, I've been through this experience many times before now!"

THEOLOGICAL NOTES

1. We simply do not know how the physical resurrection of Jesus occurred because we were not there and Jesus did not think it was important to go into the details. The stories we have in Scripture, it is generally agreed, are not detailed historical accounts, much less "instant replays." They are statements of faith. All that we can be sure of historically is that the followers of Jesus did indeed experience him as fully and completely alive many times after his death, despite their profound disinclination to do so and despite the clear changes to their own lives resulting from reporting their experience. In principle we may concede that it could have been a self-deception, but if so, its power and influence were almost as marvelous as the event itself. No useful purpose is served by arguing the fact of a historical resurrection with unbelievers. We can prove the fact of the transformation of the apostles and the fact of their belief. What we make of these facts and whether we choose to live in the light of the mystery of the cross and the resurrection are matters of deep personal choice and commitment which no one can argue.

2. Attempts to free God from the charge of being the "cause" of evil is the work of what are termed "process" theologians and philosophers. They think of God as the "Great Improviser" who respects completely the freedom of his creatures (even the freedom of the forces of nature to create its own disasters), and then subtly adjusts his plans and goals so that their fulfillment will come despite and through the exercise of creaturely freedom. The approach is interesting and persuasive, especially because it permits us to say that God suffered and died for us in and through Jesus (a traditional Christian conviction based on the custom of attributing to the divine "person" the actions of the human Jesus). The main weakness of this approach is that it seems to assume that God grows and even changes—an idea which is not false to

the scriptural data but which certainly goes against much of the philosophical and theological premises of the Christian tradition. However, the process scholars argue that growth is a perfection and hence ought to be found supremely in God (at least in what they call the "consequent nature of God"). Whether this subtle and attractive but disconcerting approach can be reconciled with the Catholic tradition is a question that will have to be answered in the future. A number of very respectable Catholic philosophical theologians have argued that a rapprochement between Thomistic theology and process theology is not only possible but absolutely necessary.

Chapter Five

THE MYSTERY OF SALVATION

Is human nature totally depraved?

(What is original sin?)

W<small>E EXPERIENCE OURSELVES AS TORN AND TWISTED. WE</small> have the best of intentions; we want to be good and generous and kind and brave, but we end up being ugly, mean, stingy, and cowardly. We are suspicious of strangers, hostile to our neighbors, disloyal to our friends, ungrateful to our parents, harsh to our spouse, unsympathetic to our children, unfaithful to our ultimate convictions.

We are filled with bad habits. We eat too much, drink too much, smoke too much, talk too much. We are uncharitable, lazy, vain, proud, irascible, nasty, unfeeling, and cruel. We don't want to be any of these things; we are ashamed of ourselves; we don't do things we want to do and we do things we don't want to do. We are creatures of passion; we fall victim to rage, hunger, fear, anxiety, depression, imperious sexuality; and yet our passions do not so completely dominate us that we do not realize at the final moment that what we are doing is shameful.

Sometimes we feel like monsters. We chastise a child who does not deserve punishment, and wince at the hurt look in his or her eyes. We are cruel and unjust to a subordinate, and sense the suppressed resentment. We lie to a superior, and feel smug but unclean. We cheat, and feel guilty in our cleverness. We reject affection from loved ones and watch their body tense with hurt. We ridicule an aging parent and see the sorrow and confusion. We are petty, ungrateful, dishonest, and vindictive. But while we know that to some extent we are trapped and do evil things because there are powerful forces of evil within our personality, we also know that any particular act of evil is gratuitous and unnecessary.

But, as monsters go, most of us are rather benign, resembling Cookie Monster of Sesame Street rather than the dread Grendel of Beowulf. We may have dropped bombs in a war, we may have killed others in combat, we may even have been a hit-and-run or drunken driver, we may have ruined someone else's reputation or career, we may be primarily responsible for a broken marriage. But we are not hit men, professional killers, assassins, concentration camp gauleiters, war criminals, child molesters, rapists, thrill killers, or psychopaths. We are not a Hitler or a Stalin; we are not responsible for the deaths of millions. Yet we know that we share the same human nature as these terrible people. We know that there are strains and tendencies in our own personality that pull us in the direction of cruelty and the destruction of others.

It is so very easy to watch complacently as a congressional committee on television picks someone apart who has been caught in violations of the law because of weakness, ambition, and fear. Yet unless we are totally caught up in our own self-righteousness, we know that we too have done similar things on a smaller scale. We have not told the truth, we have winked at the law, we have bribed, we have cut corners, we have looked the other way, we have suppressed our ethics. We have argued that "everyone is doing it."

Worse still, we are hypocrites—whiten sepulchers—all

white and shiny on the outside but filled with corruption. We pretend to be good and virtuous, to be outraged by the faults of others; yet we know that a penetrating probe of our own life would reveal in us most of the sins we denounce in others. Our morality is often an act of covering up both guilty conscience and suppressed desire.

And our desires are so powerful! In our rage we would destroy all our enemies. In our greed we would want to take everything our neighbors have. In our envy we would punish all excellence, every accomplishment, the success of someone who appears more gifted than we. In our pride we would wreck the good name of anyone who is praised. In our lust we yearn for every attractive body we see. The restraints of civilized living and our fear hold us back, but we know that within us, at times barely chained, is a wild, vicious, destructive animal.

We are filled with prejudices, biases, bad habits, and limitations. We have acquired all the narrowness of our own social class, our own ethnic group, our own neighborhood or community—sometimes without many of their virtues. We are snobs, bigots, and dogmatists; we distrust and hate those who dare to be different from us. Sometimes we try to break away from our own past, but we still carry its narrowness with us even while we try desperately to assume the limitations of the approved new class with which we try to identify.

We experience our existence as fragmented, distorted, cut off, and trapped. We are cut off from our friends, our family, those we love. We are cut off from the material world in which we live; the best we can do is use it rather than be part of it. We are cut off from that which is most generous, most authentic in us. We are cut off from our work, which for other people defines us but which to us seems strangely distant.

We are trapped in our own weakness, limitations, inherited and acquired maladies, bad temper, weak stomach, neurotic defenses, uncontrolled lust, undisciplined selfishness, thoughtless judgments, fears, anxieties, defensiveness, past mistakes, present errors, and unwise commitments. We have so little room to move, so little untrammeled freedom, so little opportunity for choice, so little chance. Caught and cut off, we live lives of routine despair.

We desire freedom and community. We often sense that we would like to break with the ingrained patterns of our past, go somewhere else and start life anew. We don't do it because we lack the courage, and perhaps because we know we would bring our problems with us. But we long to break out of the chains in which we are caught, cast them aside and start to really live. We want to belong to others and to have them belong to us, not possessively, not jealously, but honestly and freely. We want to be in contact with them; we want their support and affection and love, and we want to be able to give these in return. We want to live in peace and harmony with nature. We want to enjoy and grow in our work. We want to know and enjoy our own skills and talents and goodness. We want to have done with self-righteousness and self-pity, with arrogance and fear. We want to be ourselves.

We want liberation and reconciliation, but they seem so hard to attain. How can we escape the conclusion that human nature is either fundamentally bad or that it is caught in the chains outside forces have imposed on it?

Yet we know that neither liberation nor reconciliation is impossible to attain. If we experience our own evil, we also experience our own goodness. Sometimes our good intentions are not carried out; other times we are spontaneously and almost thoughtlessly better than we ever thought we could be. We resist an impulse to strike out at an extended helping hand, we respond to a harsh word with a heating tenderness, we bite our tongue, we restrain our passion, we choke off our rage; we yield to gentleness, sympathy, understanding, generosity, courage, and insight. We break a bad habit, conquer a vice, end a quarrel. We laugh instead of scream, relax our anxieties for a moment and give over completely to enjoyment and peace; we make love gently, skillfully, effectively, becoming momentarily one with the other, free from both resentment and inhibition. We come alive again, we are reborn, we rejoin the human race.

Liberation and reconciliation, then, are possible but never easy.

Jesus came to end man's slavery and alienation. His followers perceived themselves as both trapped and alienated (though they would not have used these words). They, like us, were sinners, hardened to their vices and bad habits. They, like us, had experienced moments of liberation and reconciliation; but when they encountered the risen Jesus, now revealed to them as Christ, they found the chains dropping away, the barriers collapsing. They were free, they were one, they could start all over again; they were reborn.

The battle between good and evil that had gone on in the personality of each of them, just as it goes on in the world, was now tilted in the direction of good. Whatever their propensities to do evil might be, they discovered that in the risen Jesus their propensities to do good were stronger. They were new men, the partisans of new, free, and reconciled humanity. They had been saved.

They strove to find figures of speech that would convey this astonishing experience of rebirth to others. The image that came most immediately to mind was the purchasing of the freedom of a slave. They had been slaves to sin and death; Jesus had purchased their freedom by his suffering and death. And they thought of the heavy debts one could acquire, debts that in their time could lead to prison and slavery. Their moral debts had been paid. God was not angry at them, they need not be angry with one another. They had been forgiven, they could forgive others. Jesus had paid their debts by his death and burial.

The word-pictures made the point. Where there had been slavery there was now freedom, where there had been a heavy burden of guilt there was now reconciliation. But the images could not be pushed too far (no image can), for in both cases they would have turned the heavenly Father into a stern and cruel judge at best and a monster at worst. In the logical absurdity of the redemption image, the Father would be presented as exacting the price of the death of his son in order to free us from the bonds of Satan. In the satisfaction image, he would have even more seriously demanded the crucifixion as a price for his injured dignity. Obviously there is no relationship between that God and the crazy farmer or the loving father of the prodigal son. Turning the picture into a metaphysical model to be taken with all literal logic converts God into exactly the opposite of what Jesus revealed to us. The liberating and reconciling God who elected to suffer in and through Jesus in order to free us and unite us ends up looking like a monster thereby.

But while God did not exact a price for our liberation, or the payment of a debt of honor in the literal meaning of those words, it was still true that the followers of Jesus experienced his death and resurrection as the cause of their liberation and reconciliation. They were free and they were one because Jesus had suffered and died. He had given them an example of how to live, he had revealed to them the love of the Father; he had shown them that evil could not conquer good, that hatred was weaker than love, that death would have to yield to life. He had shown them the "secret hidden from the ages," that God has a saving and loving plan at work in the world, that God intends that there be reconciliation and love, and that nothing would prevent the ultimate realization of this plan—not even the terrible death of the man who was most intimate with him. The cross and resurrection were necessary so that the depths of God's love might be fully shown, and so that the unshakable power of God's plan might be fully revealed. Caught up in the excitement of such love and the strength of that plan, the apostles now were themselves so excited and so strong that they could break from their chains and tear down the barriers.

Some Christians object that this does not really make Jesus the Savior. (One fears they would be content only with the image of Jesus physically opening the closed gates of heaven or physically paying off a debt to a teller in the Divine Savings and Loan Association.) In fact the cross and resurrection were essentially to release the saving dynamic of the Christ experience on the world. In the power of that dynamic it becomes possible for us to end our slavery and our alienation. We are still imprisoned and cut off, but we don't have to be. God imposes neither liberation nor reconciliation on us. The death and resurrection of Jesus neither solves our problems nor forces us to be free and united. Rather, the salvation accomplished by Jesus has made it possible for us to achieve freedom and unity by creating an environment where we know that such goals are possible, by confirming in the most vivid and dramatic way possible our own very hesitant stirrings toward liberation and reconciliation. Salvation has always been part of God's plan. Human sinfulness is an obstacle to that plan. The self-revelation of God in Jesus, and particularly in the death and resurrection of Jesus, revealed the plan. Indeed one could say that Jesus was the plan, because in him the whole plan was revealed. In this revelation we are given a new power to be liberated and reconciled because we are now able to see that our efforts to break free from the bonds of sin and overcome its constraints are integrated into God's loving graciousness. The universe is destined for freedom and reconciliation, and in Jesus we can see that such is the case and we can become part of the process. Only those who have no understanding of the power of a truth to have an immense physical impact on human life and human society will dismiss this saving revelation as merely psychological. It is much more physical in its impact (or ontological, if one likes philosophical words) than some imaginary payment at the satanic slave market or the heavenly savings and loan.

"Every man comes into the world noble and at the same time wretched, rich in a magnificent future and yet inclined to evil." The root predisposition—not yet the flaw—from which evil comes is to be found not in the fact that humankind is a composite of body and soul but rather in the fact that humankind is finite like every creature and knows its finitude, unlike any other creature save the angels. Because we are moral and are capable of reflecting on our morality, unlike any other bodily creatures, we are also capable of fear, as are all bodily creatures, and distrust— a uniquely human characteristic.

The sin of the human race is the sin of distrust—of cosmic distrust; it is the sin of refusing to believe that the universe in which we find ourselves is trustworthy and therefore the sin of refusing to believe that the power that produced the universe and placed us in it is trustworthy. Since we cannot trust the cosmos or its creator we cannot trust anyone but ourselves and hence are driven to put our security and our confidence solely in our own powers and abilities. Thus, we cannot even take the risk of treating other humans as trustworthy.

Refusing to believe in the trustworthiness of others is called hatred. Making an act of faith in the trustworthiness of others is called love. The sin of the race, therefore, is the sin of hatred. We commit our own personal sins of hatred but we are also born into a sinful race that has accumulated predispositions to hatred and the results of hatred down through the generations. The blend of our own predisposition to distrust and the accumulated distrust of the centuries is what constitutes the evil in us. But there is also the contrary and very powerful predisposition towards trusting union with others—our nature as social beings thrusts us powerfully in that direction. Thus the human personality is the arena in which conflicting forces of trust and distrust, love and hatred, fear and faith conflict. The Catholic Christian believes that there is more good than evil in human nature, more cooperation than selfishness, more trust than distrust, more love than hatred— though sometimes just barely. He believes that in the human personality there is the capacity for reconciliation, reconstruction, and restoration. Because of personal and hereditary limitations we can exercise this capacity only imperfectly, but such an exercise is by no means impossible. However, we can only engage in sustained love and reconciliation when we have first made an act of faith in the fundamental trustworthiness of the universe. In this sense, faith in God is essential to overcome the sinful dispositions of our personality and our race. Jesus came to reveal to us in a superabundance how loving is the fundamental power of the universe and hence how worthy of receiving our trust. Jesus came to tell us that we need not fear, that we could take the risk of vulnerability required by loving reconciliation. Thus it is in and through Jesus as the revelation of the loving trustworthiness of God (and the cosmos and life he has created) that we overcome the effects of the sin of the human race. The Catholic Christian today acknowledges, of course, that there are other ways of learning of God's loving trustworthiness than through Jesus. The Lord, however, is the way *par excellence*. The Catholic Christian also notes that many who do not know Jesus—and alas some who do—neither believe in the trustworthiness of life nor act like they thought it was safe to risk oneself in love.

Love for the Catholic Christian is not so much the desire to possess someone else as the desire to be possessed by the other. Love is the passionate and devout commitment of one person to the welfare and happiness of another. In such a commitment, the personal identity of the first person is not lost but enhanced because the most noble and most generous aspects of his personality are called forth. To possess another in love does not mean to be possessive of him. It means rather to graciously accept his passionate and devout commitment to my welfare and happiness, to assume that there is a tendency toward permanence in that commitment, and at the same time, to respect the radical freedom of the other. It is a risk to expose oneself to the vulnerability of such a commitment—for the other may come to reject our passionate and devout commitment. It is an equal risk to accept such a commitment (and give it in return) because respect for the radical freedom of the other leaves one open to the possibility of a devastating exercise by the other of that freedom.

We must even respect the freedom of God, though we know that he has permanently and implacably committed himself to love for us. The permanence of that commitment—like the permanence of any human commitment—is found in the freedom of God and not in any "legal" or economic claim ("possessiveness") we might wish to have on him.

The "paradise" that was "lost" by human sin is a relationship between humankind and God in which, despite our mortal, creaturely, and human propensity to fear and distrust, humans still stood in a relationship with God in which they accepted him as trustworthy and gave themselves to him in love and, through him, gave themselves to one another. Whether and how such a historic paradise may have existed, however, is not the point of Christian revelation that is concerned with the restoration of human faith in God's loving trustworthiness, through his self-revelation in Jesus—and in particular, in the death and resurrection of Jesus. (Some Catholic writers suggest that the paradise story looks both to the past events and also to the present and future opportunities which God offers humankind for reconciliation and unity—particularly through his self-disclosure in Jesus—opportunities that humankind repeatedly rejects but which God repeatedly offers again.) Such a "restoration" recreates the situation as it should be, whether or not it ever in fact had existed in the past. Reconciliation in love and trust is a fundamental longing of humankind and the basic aspiration of human nature—even if our finitude and our resulting fear and distrust impede our efforts toward such a goal. The underlying flaw in human nature, its basic and tragic weakness, its essential deprivation is that its propensity to suspicion and distrust conflicts with its propensity to openness and trust. Its self-defending hatred conflicts with its self-giving love.

So the revelation of salvation in the cross and resurrection of Jesus paradoxically confirms the fundamental goodness of human nature. Sinfulness did its worst, and then God turned the tables and revealed that, despite its best efforts to be evil, humankind was still not fundamentally depraved. For Jesus was human, and he rose from the dead; he was good, and the Father confirmed his goodness with the resurrection. And he confirms our goodness. Flawed, sinful, twisted, broken, torn, fragmented we may be, but we are still fundamentally good. Despite our sinfulness we have the capacity for salvation; we can become free and reconciled. Our unity with Jesus means that we cannot be completely depraved, and if there is any capacity for good left in us at all, then we are good; therefore—and here's the problem—we are capable of becoming better.

Catholic Christianity has always rejected both the naive optimism that denies the sinfulness of humankind and the gloomy pessimism that sees human nature as depraved. Humankind, in the Catholic view of things, is basically good but capable of terrible depravities. Through the ages of its existence it has shown itself to be depraved and sinful indeed, and this tendency keeps humankind from being all that it can be, all that it wants to be, and all that it was meant to be. Still the evil disposition of humankind does not make it evil in itself. On the contrary, the basic goodness is still latent in human nature, waiting to be freed. So, unlike traditional Protestantism, Catholic Christianity does not believe that Jesus merely covers over human sinfulness. Catholic Christianity does not believe that humankind by itself could have broken with its sinful past; it needs the revelation of God's salvation in the cross and resurrection of Jesus. Unlike such writers as Rousseau, Marx, and Freud, Catholic Christianity does not believe that human sinfulness is merely the result of political, economic, or psychological oppression; it is convinced that human sinfulness is much deeper than that. But neither does Catholic Christianity deny the importance of political, economic, and psychological oppression as both cause and effect of sinfulness; it tells its members that the struggle against these oppressions is part of God's saving plan—which now, as in the time of Jesus, needs our cooperation. Finally, Catholic Christianity rejects the notion preached by some present-day pessimists—and practiced on occasion by some of its own leaders—that you cannot trust humans to be free, because in their freedom they will destroy themselves. Catholic Christianity is under no illusion about human sinfulness and does not think that progress against its effects will be quick or easy. But it does believe that God created humankind as good and that He plans for the triumph of that goodness. The victory that Jesus won over sin and death was a revelation, not only of the goodness of God but of the goodness of humankind, which was created in the image and likeness of God.

The victory of Jesus was not won without suffering. Neither will our own personal victories be won without suffering. We will wrestle with our evil tendencies up to and beyond death. The victory of Jesus gives us the courage to stay at the battle no matter how many times we are repulsed. Nor will the victory of humankind over its collective evil be quick in coming. It, too, will have to be "purchased" at the cost of much hard work, suffering, commitment, failure, and rededication. But the Catholic Christian knows that the victory will be won because of the decisive victory of Jesus. And that means that as much as we would like to, as weary as we get, as many failures as we experience, we cannot quit.

The Christian never quits in the fight against evil. And that is as good a description of him as any.

THEOLOGICAL NOTES

1. Adam, theologians agree, is used in the Scriptures as both an individual and as a corporate personality. The sin of Adam, then, is both individual and corporate. In the past, perhaps too much emphasis has been placed on the individual aspect of this sinfulness and not enough on its corporate nature. Humankind as a collectivity is sinful—as one need only read the morning papers to observe. We are born into a race that has piled up a terrible record of sins throughout its past, and that record is part of our cultural and psychic inheritance. In a very real sense the sins of parents are visited upon their children, because the children's personalities are so much the result of parental behavior and the cultural influences of the society in which children are born. It is a badly flawed heritage that is passed on to us. It is a critically defective human race into which we come. The sinfulness began with the beginning of the human race and has gone on until now. The result is a heritage burdened with evil. However, countervailing forces of good have also been at work, alleviating the burden if not eliminating it.

The real problem is not why our first parents sinned, but why there is sin at all. This is the restatement in the human domain of the mystery of evil, or more properly the mystery of good and evil. While the mystery cannot be resolved, we must at least say that in the case of the human creature, the capacity for freedom made necessary the possibility of evil.

2. The early Christian writers—St. Irenaeus in particular—heavily emphasized the victory aspect of salvation. *Christus Victor* ("Christ the Victor") seemed to be the best way to describe what the Easter event revealed about human sinfulness. Contemporary theologians, made uneasy by the absurdities (frequently offensive to both non-Christians and thoughtful Christians alike) to which the redemption and satisfaction images can be pushed when they

are turned into literal theological paradigms, are beginning once again to emphasize the victory picture—an emphasis that seems especially appropriate in our own gloomy and pessimistic era, when fear of the destructive aspects of humankind almost paralyzes many people.

3. Catholic social theory does not think you can remake human nature by changing its social and economic environment. Yet it is committed to such change because a more open and just human society frees the individual to make more of his own personal decisions about liberation and reconciliation. In particular it does not believe that an all-powerful state can produce a new kind of human within a generation. Neither does it believe, as does the old liberal rationalism, that society is made up of struggling, antagonistic, isolated individuals. Human nature, in the view of Catholic social theory, is not nearly as pliable as the Marxists believe, and not nearly as individualistic and selfish as the rationalists and some Protestants seem to believe. Humans are fundamentally good and fair and cooperative unless they are afraid. Salvation is God's revelation that there is nothing of which we ultimately need be afraid. Catholic social commitment means working for a social and political and economic order where the causes of fear are steadily diminished.

Chapter Six

The Mystery of Grace

Can our guilt be wiped away?

(What is sanctifying grace?)

W<small>E ARE GUILTY. INDEED, WE ARE HOUNDED, TORMENTED,</small> plagued, overwhelmed by our guilt. Some of it is related to things that we did when we knew we were wrong. We cheated on a test; teased another person mercilessly; stole from a supermarket; lied to a teacher, a parent, a friend. We swore a false oath, we consciously gave a bad piece of advice, we were not fair to a child, we were ungrateful to a parent. We bribed a public official, we disillusioned a young admirer, we subtly but effectively undermined the self-esteem of another, we mistreated a neighbor. We had a serious auto accident because we were drunk. We flirted with another woman's husband, tried to seduce another man's wife, harassed a woman whose job depended on us, tempted a man whose weakness could lead to our progress.

We try to kid ourselves about these actions. We argue that everyone did them, that no one was hurt, or that they were not really wrong. More generally we blame the cultural mores of the moment or the unfairness of the world that rewards those who take what they can get. But deep down inside we know that we were responsible for doing something wrong. The deed is done, we may be sorry for it, or at least we may regret the harm that followed; but we did it nevertheless, and we are guilty.

There are other areas of guilt for which we are not clearly responsible personally. There is hunger and injustice in the world, racism in our country, cruelty in our prison systems, war being waged all over the world, inequality in our places of business.

It is not enough for some of us that we want to correct the injuries and injustices of the past, or that we are doing all we can to improve conditions for the poor and the oppressed in the present. We must feel collective guilt (which is often more powerful than the guilt we feel for being unkind to our children or harsh to our spouse or inconsiderate of a neighbor). And of course it is somehow more comfortable to feel the overwhelming guilt about what is separate from us in time and space than it is to feel guilty about something we did to someone close to us.

Oftentimes these social guilts result from an even vaguer free-floating guilt that drifts around in our personality looking for something to fasten itself to. We are guilty and we do not know precisely why. Somehow we have failed, we have let people down, we are not good enough, we haven't been able to live up to our talents or to other people's expectations. We are, we fear, no good at all.

All of us experience some self-hatred; all of us engage in self-punishment. Many of us cannot stand ourselves and wish desperately that we were someone else. We spend much of our time punishing ourselves for our own worthlessness, sometimes by compulsive and obsessive behavior and other times by cruelty to those who love us. For some of us, self-hatred is so powerful that we slowly destroy ourselves by overworking, overeating, overdrinking, and drug addiction. We devote our whole lives to punishing our own contemptible worthlessness. A few people are so filled with self-loathing that they inflict the ultimate punishment of suicide on themselves.

Some guilt is real, other guilt is neurotic, and much of our guilt is a complex combination of the two. In practice, guilt feels pretty much the same whatever the cause. It makes us feel low, mean, miserable, despicable. How can anyone possibly love us when they know or can find out what we are really like? It often seems to us that such filth should be wiped off the face of the earth. We have betrayed just about everyone.

And yet we are aware of the possibility of healing and forgiveness. Our mother catches us stealing the cookies, listens to the obvious lie, and then sighs, smiles, shakes her head, and asks us not to do it again. Unaccountably and undeservedly, we have been forgiven. We forget a critical birthday or anniversary and the offended party just laughs it off with some comment about how much we have on our minds. Again, for some strange reason we have been forgiven. We draw a complete blank about attending a party and we are invited back. We blow an important responsibility and the boss or the client shrugs it off and says that we don't do that sort of thing very often so it's all right. We do our best to pick a fight with a loved one and the other overcomes us with tenderness. We are unfair to a child and the little one brings us a present.

Despite our guilty behavior, then, the other person refuses to hold us guilty. The objective fact of what we have done is still there, but the other graciously dismisses it as unimportant to the continuation of the relationship. The other person basically likes us and forgives us easily, readily, charmingly, because of the affection he has for us. Love bears no ill will.

In the Christ event the followers of Jesus learned that God is gracious toward us, that he does not hold our moral ugliness against us, and that he forgives quickly and easily, almost before we get around to asking him. He does so for the same reason a parent forgives the child who steals the cookies or a spouse forgives an erring partner: he loves us. In the light of their Easter experience the followers of Jesus saw clearly what he tried to drive home in parables like the story of the loving father and the prodigal son: God is almost pathetically eager to have us back. He forgives us even when we are unable to forgive ourselves. We can no more merit his forgiving love than we can merit existence. It is there ready for us to accept it. You cannot earn what is there for the asking.

The apostles now understood the meaning of the parable of the good shepherd who foolishly left his flock to pursue one worthless and stupid little lamb, and the parable of the crazy woman who invited all her neighbors to a party to celebrate the recovery of an almost worthless coin. By human standards, the readiness of God to forgive is crazy.

The followers of Jesus especially understood the way Jesus responded to the woman taken in adultery. One by one her accusers drop away before the demand that the sinless one among them begin the stoning. Then, turning to this shameful, trembling, vile woman, he calmly asks whether there is anyone left to accuse her. When she replies, "No one, Lord," he sends her on her way to begin life again. "Go and sin no more." Pardon given without petition, absolution given without confession, remission of guilt without entreaty. It would be a terrible way to run a human legal system, but it is the way God works.

When the followers of Jesus looked for a name to attach to this forgiving love, it had to be from the Greek language, because most of their writing and preaching outside of Palestine was in Greek. They chose the word *charis*, which we translate as "grace." Unfortunately the word has been so badly kicked around in theological controversy that another word, like "graciousness" or even "gracefulness," would convey better the kind of meaning about God we mean. When we speak of "graceful" we could mean, for example, a charming hostess, a woman of taste, elegance, sensitivity, who is skillful at putting her guests at ease, making them feel at home, and drawing out the best of them with her sparkling conversation. She doesn't have to do these things, of course; it is enough that she plans the party, invites the guests, purchases the food and drink, and serves it to them; but her grace is so impressive that when the guests leave they remember only the charm of their hostess.

St. Paul, in his many different writings on grace (and, as is often the case with a new term, he uses it in many different senses), says that grace is the characteristic that marks God's dealings with people. His love is not forced by our actions, his forgiveness is not merited by our goodness, and his affection is not won by our careful, punctilious obedience to the law. God is not an accountant carefully keeping the books, not a judge looking for grounds in the law to convict, not a teller diligently counting our merits. On the contrary, God acts with grace; he gives himself to us with unrestrained and sovereign generosity, asking only an equally unrestrained response from us. God intends that God and man shall meet in a communion of mutual giving and receiving. Grace, then, is God's gift of himself to us; it is God giving himself to us.

In the New Testament the word *grace* is often used in the broadest sense. It covers the whole of God's gift of himself to man. Grace is not merely one on a long list of God's gifts, it is rather the whole list; and since the whole list is summarized in God's revelation of himself through Jesus, Jesus is the gift *par excellence*. The union of God and man in Jesus is grace *par excellence*.

It is true that God's relationship with humankind has always been grace, but in the life, death, and resurrection of Jesus that grace is revealed in so overwhelming and special a way that one can say, not merely that the whole of God's purpose and plan is told to us in Jesus, but that the sum of God's love is offered to us in Jesus.

If grace *is* God—and this is surely what is meant in the New Testament—then we receive God in his gift-giving; and he expects to receive us back in return. It is an exchange of gifts much like the exchange of bodies between husband and wife in the marriage act—a comparison that did not escape St. Paul. Just as an earthly lover makes a total gift of self in love and expects the total gift of the other in return, so God expects a complete response to his complete gift. Between human lovers there is no barter, no legalism, no careful counting of obligations, and so with God; there is graciousness in the relationship between God and man. Spontaneity, generosity, and self-forgetfulness are the signs of authentic love between humans, and so are they the marks of God's love for us.

In the Greek Christian tradition there has been considerable emphasis on the "deification" aspects of grace. By giving himself to us, God establishes a union with us, and in this union we come to belong to God. The union of man and God in Jesus is but a special example of the union that is available to all humans who are willing to respond "gracefully" to God's offer of love. Grace is humankind's union with God; indeed it is humankind united to God.

Such language smacks of mysticism; and well it might, because many of the people who used it—like St. Paul—were mystics. They had experienced that intense and ecstatic interlude in which the personality seems to be lifted out of itself and united with a powerful, generous, self-giving love that is perceived as animating the universe. Such experiences are not infrequent even in our day, and they can be described quite literally as grace, an experience of intimate and intensely pleasurable union with That Which Is.

But even for those of us who have no such spectacular interludes in our lives, the mystery of grace reveals to us that we are lovable beyond our wildest imaginings. The forgiveness we experience almost every day from those who love us is a hint of the grace that is at work in the universe. The healing we feel in a warm, generous, passionate act of human love is but a faint reflection of the healing that is actively pursuing us wherever we go.

The Hound of Heaven that the poet Francis Thompson wrote of more than one hundred years ago in describing God may be after us with implacable "unperturbed pace," but it is a loving gentle, tender pursuit that seeks only to give us all that there is and to be united with us in mutual generosity.

It is arguable, of course, that the universe is not that way at all. But we have hints that it is: in the ecstatic graciousness of mystical interludes, in the ordinary graciousness of normal experiences of delight and joy, and in that very special graciousness of healing and forgiving human love. Christians believe that the mystery of God's forgiving, uniting, reconciling grace revealed to us in the Christ event confirms these hints. We are not alone, after all; there is love out there and it wants us. Indeed if the mystery of grace is to be accepted, it wants us with the kind of insistent passion that makes the pursuit of a beloved by a sexually aroused lover look tame by comparison. How then do we act in response? How does one react to a charming and gracious hostess? We yield to her charm. We forget our worries, our resentments, our envy, our nastiness, and we give ourselves over to enjoying the party. So the only way to surrender to God's forgiving love is to give ourselves over to it.

We must also, it appears, work rather vigorously on our own self-esteem. For reasons that escape us completely, the animating power of the universe claims to have fallen in love with us. By our own standards we are usually not very lovable and don't deserve forgiveness. We should be left to rot in the corruption of our own filth; we should be weighted down forever with the insupportable burden of our guilt. But That Which Is, the Something Else out there, seems to have other plans. He seems to find us immensely lovable. So we must accept that we are far better than we think we are, and we must treat our battered, guilt-ridden, self-hating, self-rejecting personality with more respect and affection than we have in the past.

And of course we must forgive others—which may be the

biggest catch of all. "Forgive us our trespasses as we forgive those who trespass against us. " We may say it every day, but we usually don't mean it. If God should measure his standards of forgiveness by those we follow, we would be in very bad straits indeed. Lord deliver us from our just desserts.

The story of the unjust steward is powerful evidence of what God expects. Having been forgiven a huge debt by his master, the steward then turned around and had a colleague tossed into jail for a trifling sum that the man owed him. When the master found out, things went badly for the steward. He had not got the point of the master's message: loving forgiveness should lead to more loving forgiveness. It is not merely a matter of good example. Grace extended creates an environment in which we in turn can be gracious to others. The forgiven child knows that there is enough love in the home to go around, and he does not have to be harsh with his baby sister. If the animating power of the universe forgives us all our guilt, then we know the world in which we live is gracious enough that we can afford to run the risk of not holding grudges against others.

Loving forgiveness is contagious.

THEOLOGICAL NOTES

1. Theologians have always distinguished between *uncreated grace* and *created grace*—the former being God's free and generous gift of self, the latter being the effect in the human personality of that gift. Among Greek Christians the emphasis has tended to be on the former, and among Latin Christians, the latter. (This is for reasons having to do with the theological history of both areas—in particular the dominant influence of St. Augustine in the West, and through him the Reformation controversies.) However, at the present time it is generally agreed that the conditions in which we find ourselves call for a return in the West to

the older Greek emphasis, an emphasis that is reflected in the preceding interpretation of the mystery of grace.

2. Since the Middle Ages there has also been a frequent distinction made between *sanctifying grace* (God's basic gift of himself) and *actual grace* (his support for us in individual actions). Theologians rightfully have wondered about the importance of such a distinction, because God's gift of himself to us is total and complete, even though it may manifest itself in many different ways at different times in our lives.

Chapter Seven

THE MYSTERY OF THE HOLY EUCHARIST

Is it possible to have friends?

(Is Jesus really present in the Holy Eucharist?)

Iₙ OUR SEARCH FOR COMMUNITY WITH OTHERS WE ARE OFTEN at odds with our fellow humans. We want the warmth and support of friendship but we frequently find ourselves fighting with those who are our friends.

Our parents bring us into the world. They feed, clothe, and protect us while we are helpless and defenseless, and yet from our first selfish wail as a neonate we struggle with them, demanding both their service and our freedom from their control. Our brothers and sisters are the closest people in the world to us, yet we compete with them for parental attention and affection as children, and often we continue these sibling rivalries into adult life. Our classmates in school are our allies against the "establishment" of parental and school regulations, yet the atmosphere of childhood and adolescent peer groups is frequently poisoned by envy and dominated by a narrowness and rigidity that permits little deviation from its strict norms. We spend much of the day with our work colleagues, and yet rivalry, envy, and competition often dominate our relationships with them. We will unite with our neighbors to defend the community against outside attack, but suspicion and distrust, as well as competition and envy, grow like weeds even on the most carefully landscaped blocks. We give our life, body and soul, to our spouse, but we hold back just enough so that in the home and in the marriage bed we feel like we are in an armed camp. And finally, to our sorrow, we find our children punishing us just as we punished our parents for living so close to us, loving us so much, and getting old. We search for community, we long for communion, and yet we are usually unfulfilled, often ending up in pain and suffering.

Still we do experience friendship often enough to know that it is possible among humans. Indeed, in those moments of communion, we suspect that self-giving affection is the only authentically human way to live.

In friendship, particularly in married friendship, we find that we are taken out of ourselves and united with the other. The experience is not usually as intense as the mystical interlude, but it is very strong nevertheless. In the highest moments of human friendship we forget about ourselves and we leave behind our fears, our inhibitions, our restraints; we remain fully who we are. Indeed we are more fully ourselves at those times than at most other times, and yet we exist for and through and in the other person. We are concerned about them in a way that we normally reserve for ourselves, and we are able to be ourselves for them in a way that is impossible in other circumstances. Despite the emotional intensity of such friendship, we do not grow weary from it. On the contrary, such communion relaxes and invigorates us. Instead of producing nervousness, uncertainty, and anxiety, interludes with our friends make us serene and self-confident. We go back to our other relationships with our esteem restored, our fears quieted, our eyes clear, and our hearts light. We are loved.

Such interludes are all too short. "O slowly, slowly run, you steeds of night" said a Roman poet about his awareness that all would be dissipated in the cold light of day. Still the experience of being loved and giving oneself in love in return is so rewarding that we are forced to believe that this is the way humans were meant to live.

The followers of Jesus experienced him as their friend. He said explicitly, "I do not call you servants, I call you friends." In spite of their competitions and rivalries, they still found that being part of his band of brothers was the most exciting and challenging experience of their lives. Their hearts burned within them, as the two disciples who met Jesus on the road to Emmaus said. When they were with Jesus the apostles found that they were freer to be themselves than in any other circumstances. In the warmth of the attractiveness that flowed from Jesus it was not necessary—and was a waste of time—to pretend, to defend, to hide. Jesus seemed capable of complete dedication to them, and in their own narrow and unperceptive fashion, they responded with dedication of their own.

The high points of their years together were their community meals. Reclining around a table as the light faded after the labors of the day, they became conscious of their union with one another and with Jesus and his work, whatever that work might be. All Jewish meals had a certain ritual about them; they were all "mini" Passover dinners, they were all "thanksgivings" for the food they were in the process of eating and for the immense benefits the Lord Yahweh had bestowed upon his people. In their simple, relaxed, and, one supposes, frequently quite crude dinners together, the apostles gave thanks to God for the opportunity to be together with Jesus and with one another. The common meal was a celebration of their community, a reinforcement of it, and an expression of gratitude for its continued existence.

It was especially in such common meals that they were aware of the gift Jesus had made of himself to them. Indeed, in their last supper together Jesus went so far as to perform the task of a slave and wash their feet. In their Easter experience of the risen Lord they perceived what these common meals had meant. Not only had Jesus given himself to them, Jesus was a gift from God; he was God's self-revelation. In the life of Jesus, and especially in those interludes of intense friendship at the common meal, God had given himself to them. In the evening meals with Jesus, there had been communion between God and man. Now they understood what Jesus had meant when at the last of these meals together he had taken ordinary bread and ordinary wine and had identified himself with them. Now they realized what Jesus meant when he instructed them to continue these dinners in memory of him. The communion between God and man would continue at their common meals, because even though he was no longer visible to them Jesus would still be with them when they came together for the breaking of the bread and the drinking of the wine. And they would still give thanks to the Father in heaven for the gift of communion between themselves and God, as made known and revealed in Jesus.

So the common meals continued and became the central activity of the early Christian community. When they gathered to break bread together, they celebrated their communion with one another, and Jesus was present once again in their midst.

Humans have always had rituals in their religion. The idea was that when they came together to "celebrate the mysteries" they united themselves with the great saving events of the past from which their religion came. In their rituals they found communion with the deity who had revealed himself in these events, and they continued them and applied their power to their own lives. The great fertility rites of the nature religions of primitive cultures reenacted the primordial events which had brought life and vitality to the earth and linked the planting of crops, the tilling of the fields, the taking in of the harvest—ordinary activities on which the village depended for its life—with the great events of creation. The God who had produced life was present again in such rituals, continuing his work for the people. And thus his people ordered the life of the fields and cooperated with him in bringing forth the rich and fertile abundance of the harvest.

So there was nothing unique about the Christian notion that they could have communion with God, reenact his saving deeds, and continue his work through ritual. Nor were they the first to turn a spring festival into a celebration ritual that commemorated God's generous gift of life to his people. (In its origin, the Passover dinner itself was a spring fertility festival—the unleavened bread coming from the agricultural past of the people and the paschal lamb from its more distant pastoral years.) Nor did they invent the idea of a ritual dinner at which God or his representative was the guest, unseen but present for those who believed. Human religions abound with ritual meals, and many of the Jewish sects (such as those who lived in the monasteries by the Dead Sea) had much more elaborate ritual dinners than did the followers of Jesus.

The difference in the Christian ritual supper was not its form or its style but the events it remembered and continued and also the God whose presence was celebrated and with whom Holy Communion was kept. The events remembered and continued were the life, death, and resurrection of the same Jesus who had once reclined around the table with them (and in the earliest days, it was doubtless around the very same table). The God with whom they communed was the passionately loving, eagerly forgiving, gracious God who had given himself to them through his gift of Jesus. The Christians celebrated at the "Lord's supper" the gift of Jesus who was now present among them again though in an unseen way. They rejoiced at the incredibly good news that Jesus had brought them, that our fleeting hints about the graciousness that seems to animate the universe were true beyond our wildest dreams. They commemorated and reenacted the great events of their lives together with Jesus, they ratified and reinforced their communion with one another through Jesus; and then they went forth to their difficult and dangerous lives, strengthened, encouraged, and invigorated for the work that was still to be done. They had taken both physical and spiritual nourishment from their meal together, and for it all they gave thanks, explicitly at the end of the meal but also and more importantly through the fact of the meal itself. Very early the meal of the Lord's Supper became known also by another name that emphasized its thanksgiving aspect—the Eucharist (from the Greek work meaning "thanksgiving").

All of this was natural and unselfconscious. They continued a custom that had begun with Jesus; they kept alive a tradition of ritual meals that had come down from their ancestors and that other strains of the heterogeneous religious pluralism of Second Temple Judaism also practiced. They gave thanks, they celebrated their unity with one another. Elaborate ceremony and even more elaborate religious reflection and theologizing would come later. Neither the ceremony nor the theology is necessarily bad, and both of them are certainly inevitable developments; but they become pernicious accretions when they destroy the simple fact that the Eucharist is a friendship supper eaten together by a group of human beings who share a common cause and have received a common gift, the self-disclosure of God in Jesus. The Eucharist is a common meal eaten by those who are united through Jesus in love for one another. The Eucharist is a ritual commitment to the possibility of unity in friendship among human beings.

Eating with a person is an act of great intimacy. For reasons that probably have to do with the dangers around the campfire in front of the caves of our prehistoric past, one normally shares a meal only with someone who is trusted. To invite a person to eat with one is a mark of trust, confidence, and affection; to accept an invitation is to return the same sentiments. There is an atmosphere of relaxation and enjoyment about the act of eating that, in principle at least, makes it the kind of act we share only with those we trust or love. We do not like to eat alone. We are ill at ease eating with strangers. We enjoy supper with our friends and family. A common meal is a sign of our intimacy, and it is attended with the vulnerability intimacy involves.

Common meals do not always work out that way. St. Paul had trouble with the Christians of Corinth who had become contentious and unruly scarcely a few decades after the death of Jesus. Our family suppers all too easily turn into chaos or intervals of silent-but-bitter reproach. Our great family dinners at Thanksgiving and Christmas are often times when old wounds are opened and new wounds inflicted. But the reason for the easy corruptibility of the common meal is that we can hardly prevent ourselves from coming to it with great expectations. It is that moment at the end of the day or during the busy time of year in which we can slow down, relax, enjoy one another with ease and graciousness, to celebrate the love we feel for each other. Unfortunately there often isn't any love to celebrate.

The followers of Jesus were not likely to forget that at the Last Supper Jesus washed their feet. Nor were they likely to forget that on the next day he suffered and died for them. God, through Jesus, had revealed a love for his creatures that meant that he would serve them. The secret of keeping the community together after Jesus had gone would be to continue this generous, self-giving service that, in Jesus, reflected the love of the heavenly Father for all his creatures. If God had served unselfishly, so must they. That is the secret of sustaining friendship. One keeps an intimate relationship going by calculating, not ways of getting but ways of giving. One sustains affection, not by being served but by serving. One keeps the fires of love burning hot and bright, not by thinking about oneself but by being concerned with the good of the other. Paradoxically, one gets the most for oneself by being the most unselfish. Only he who gives himself generously to another can expect any generosity in return. The aim of love is not to possess the other but to be possessed by the other.

This is what the Christian Eucharist was supposed to be.

Having received the gift of God in Jesus, Christians give themselves to one another. The warmth and generosity of the Christian ritual meal was supposed to spill out and transform all the other common meals in which a Christian participated—particularly those with the ones he loved the most.

It is obvious that such a transformation does not always occur. The imagery of the Eucharist has been obscured, and many people do not realize what they are about when they take part in it. But this may not be the basic problem. The imagery was quite clear to the Christians of Corinth, yet we have Paul's testimony that they were still able to ignore it and continue fighting with one another. If the Eucharist does not transform completely the atmosphere of the other common meals that Christians eat, the reason is not that the message of the Eucharist is obscure. It is rather that the message of friendship through self-forgetting sacrifice is one we would much prefer not to receive. It has not been tried and found wanting; it has been found hard and not tried.

The Last Supper was connected (there is some debate about how) with the Jewish Passover. A purified spring fertility rite, the Passover celebrated the liberating and life-giving love of Yahweh for his people in the past. Holy Communion (or the Mass) is a paschal banquet, an Easter dinner. It is Easter every day of the year; for it celebrates, commemorates, and represents the Christ event that the followers of Jesus experienced on the first day of the week. It is the Easter experience all over again.

It also may be thought of as a wedding banquet in which the union between God and his people is celebrated. We mark great events in our lives with splendid meals. The nuptials between God and his people took place when God gave himself completely for his people (as a husband and wife give themselves completely for and to one another in marriage) in the summing-up acts of the last three days of Holy Week. The Mass is a wedding banquet precisely because it is Easter every day of the year.

The Eucharist, then, is the center of the Christian life because it is the ritual that contains in one package all the mysteries we have so far described—God, Jesus, Holy Spirit, cross and resurrection, salvation, and grace. If one wants to know what Christians believe about the nature and purpose of our existence, one need only consider the Eucharist. Life is about love—joyous, intense, generous, and self-giving love—that seeks not to be served but to serve others. God invites us to love by giving himself to us, and we respond by giving ourselves to him in the loving service of others. Holy Communion is not merely the reception of the host; it is a whole style of living. It is, like the rest of Christianity, not the performance of certain actions but rather a style of performing all actions, a style of generous, celebrating joy.

The Sunday Holy Communion of Christians may not always look very joyous or very generous or very loving. But then Jesus never expected perfection from his followers (a good thing, because he never got it). He does expect effort, effort at making the Eucharist a joyous, generous event, and effort at transferring the joy and generosity to all our common meals and to all the intimate relationships which are commemorated, and hopefully strengthened, in such meals.

THEOLOGICAL NOTE

Jesus identified himself with bread and wine. Christians have never doubted that Jesus was really present in the Eucharist, although some of the explanations they gave for the "how" of this presence have been deemed unacceptable as means of safeguarding the "fact" of the presence. In the first thousand years the explanations were mostly drawn from Platonic philosophy. Jesus was present in the Eucharist, St. Augustine told us (in words which would have doubtless got him into trouble in a later age if people were not careful to grasp his meaning properly) *per modum symboli*—in the manner of a symbol. He meant, of course, that Jesus was present in the Eucharist the way a platonic "idea" was present in a concrete particular. In a later and more Aristotelian era, the word *transubstantiation* ("change of substance") was used to convey the same or a similar idea. At the Council of Trent the word *transubstantiation* was used to defend the real presence of Jesus against some of the reformers who seemed not to sufficiently safeguard the fact of that reality to the Council fathers. (Whether they misunderstood what the reformers were about is another matter, and is not appropriate for this book.) However, the Council certainly did not intend to define the Aristotelian philosophy or physics on which the word was based. Contemporary theologians are struggling for a new set of philosophical terms that can explain the "how" of the real presence in words that our own era can grasp. However, it would be a mistake for a Christian to become so obsessed with the "how" of the real presence as to forget about the "fact"—especially the challenging implications and demands of that fact—and to ignore in his own life the "why."

LITURGICAL NOTE

The purpose of the reforms in the liturgy of the Second Vatican Council was to make much clearer to the Christian people the richness of the mystery of the Holy Eucharist. It had looked much like an obscure (not to say on occasion a bizarre) performance that they attended as an onlooking audience. Now it is much more clearly a common commemorative action in which the people participate as full-fledged partners. The reforms have been accepted with approval by some seven-eighths of the Catholic population; but, it still must be said that Mass in a large church with a great number of people does not look much like a common meal at the end of the day with a tiny band of friends. Some of the "house" liturgies that have become common, however, seem to convey this core symbolism much more adequately. The Eucharist is always the ritual activity of the *local church*, even if on occasion it is celebrated by people from many different localities. It is rooted in the ground of a particular place, as every meal must necessarily be. You do not eat dinner in the whole world, you eat it in your home and then go forth into the world.

Chapter Eight

THE MYSTERY OF THE CHURCH

Can there be unity among humankind?

(Is there salvation outside the Catholic Church?)

H UMANKIND SEEMS TO BE IN THE PROCESS OF DESTROYING itself. We are one species, it would seem, yet unlike most animals we kill our own kind at a prodigious rate. Some anthropologists suggest that we do so because there are many varieties of humans whom we don't recognize as humans like ourselves. In other creatures recognition of conspecifics is programmed into the nervous system. Humans have to learn to recognize another as a fellow. Apparently we are not very good at learning.

One need only read the record of the bloody thirty years since the end of the worst war in human history to know that scientific progress has not eliminated mass murder. The list of killers is endless: Hindus and Muslims at the time of the partition of British India; Communists (usually non-Moslem) and non-Communists in Indonesia; Tamils and Sinhalese in Sri Lanka (Ceylon); light-skinned Muslims and dark-skinned Muslims in Bangladesh; Kurds and Iraqi in the Middle East; Arabs and blacks in the Sudan; Ibo and Yoruba in Nigeria; Tutsi and Tutu in Ruanda-Urundi; Arab and Jew in Palestine (both

Semitic peoples, be it noted); Turk and Greek on Cyprus; Protestant and Catholic in Ulster. These conflicts represent perhaps twenty million people killed, and most of them never make the front pages of our newspapers. One need not go back very far to find six million Jews and twelve million Russians killed by the Nazis, several million Armenians killed by the Turks, and between two and three million Irish permitted to die of starvation by the British during the various famines of the eighteenth and nineteenth centuries.

Black and white in the United States; French and English in Canada; Great Russians and the lesser nationalities in the Soviet Union; Han Chinese and Tibetans in China; Scottish, Welsh, and English in the island of Britain; Basque and Spanish in Spain; Norman, Breton, and Provencal in France, Fleming and Walloon in Belgium; Indian and native in the Fiji Islands; Indian and black in some Caribbean countries; white, black, and Indian in South Africa—the list of tense situations and possible flash points could go on almost indefinitely.

Nice people, these humans.

Yet we can get along well enough with each other as individuals. The "some of my best friends are . . ." line is now taken to be a mark of the bigot, but even the bigot has to acknowledge the universal human experience of fellow feeling toward those who are technically our sworn enemies. In his remarkable interviews with "middle Americans," Robert Coles quotes long paragraphs of what sounds like the most blatant racism from a white policeman, but then the interview ended with the officer saying, ". . . but I don't blame them. If I were black, I'd do the same thing."

It is a most astonishing thing to discover that someone we are supposed to hate has the same hopes, the same fears, the same aspirations for himself and his family that we do. He is not supposed to be that way at all. A white woman who has learned to be afraid of a black neighborhood is astonished to discover that black women are every bit as much afraid of the same neighborhood. A Christian who is brought up to believe that Jews have no morals is astonished when a Jewish colleague agonizes over moral decisions. A Protestant and a Catholic in Ulster discover to their amazement that they are both delighted when an Ulster team beats a south of Ireland team in a rugby match. A professor is astonished when he discovers that beneath the inarticulate language of a cab driver is a very sophisticated view of human nature.

In these revelatory experiences we discover to our astonishment that the stranger is in fact a brother or a sister, and we exclaim in surprise, "Why, they're just like us!" Such fellow feeling does not end conflict, and merely getting to know others is not a solution to national or international problems. But the revelation of fellow feeling does tell us that humankind was meant to live together in peace and harmony, and that something has gone terribly wrong in our relationships with one another. We want peace and reconciliation, but we do not seem able to find them.

Jesus worked almost entirely with Jews. Yet there was an obvious universalism in his message. If God was giving himself to humankind, there could obviously be no limitations imposed on the extent of that gift. If in Jesus humanity was to be re-created, as it had been created in the first Adam, then the conflicts that separated the various kinds of humans were to be eliminated as part of this new creation. The kingdom of God was for the whole world.

In the account we have of the ecstatic experience of Pentecost (part of the whole Easter interlude in the lives of the followers of Jesus), it became clear that the differences that separated humankind were to be no barrier to the Gospel. The Parthians and the Medes, the Cappadocians and the Elamites, all heard the preaching of the apostles, but each in their own language. Whatever the precise nature of that event historically, it surely came to mean for the early Christians that the Good News was for everyone and would know no obstacles of language or nationality. Later, after the followers of Jesus had painfully clarified how this insight would apply to the case of relationships between Jew and Gentile within their number, St. Paul could claim, "Neither Jew nor Gentile, neither Greek nor Roman, neither male nor female but all one in Christ Jesus."

This "catholicity" of the Good News did not mean the elimination of differences. A common language did not replace the individual languages of the Pentecostal participants; rather language differences simply did not stand in the way of the Good News. Similarly, Paul was wise enough to know that Greeks and Romans would not forsake their cultural traditions to form some overarching compromise culture. And he hardly expected the biological differences between man and woman to vanish. His point was that such differences would not stand in the way of the unity of humankind in Jesus. Part of the gift of God to humans in Jesus was the gift of the restoration of unity, a gift that has to be freely accepted, of course.

It need hardly be noted that that acceptance is far from complete.

So for the early followers of Jesus the "assembly of the faithful" (*ecclesia* or "church") was in principle the whole of humanity restored to unity in Jesus. The writers of the second century were incredibly universalist in their orientation: anything that was good, anything that was true, anything that was beautiful was welcome in the Christian community no matter what the cultural source. In the exuberance of the still fresh Christ experience, they were hardly ready to draw narrow and tight boundaries, and were completely unthreatened by fears of losing the uniqueness of their message. Hence they were able to transform many pagan customs (a practice that would have horrified their Jewish predecessors). If all humans were brothers and sisters in Jesus, whatever was good in the customs of any human could be welcome among the followers of Jesus. In this sense, Christianity was "catholic" (or universal) from the very beginning. It was for everyone and, in principle, open to everything.

So, then, the assembly was potentially the whole of humankind, and actually, for the moment, that segment of humankind that had heard the Good News of the Christ event was responding to it. The actual Church was nothing more and nothing less than the band of those who had heard of the Easter event, felt the Christ experience themselves, and now intended to live the brightness of its light, giving themselves to others with the same generosity with which God had given himself to us in Jesus.

But the response of humans to Jesus did not take place either as a collection of isolated individuals or as a global mass. The assembly existed wherever the Lord's Supper was celebrated. The memory of the intimacy of the Jesus experience was far too strong for his followers ever to let the warmth and power of such small communities slip away. The Eucharist was the public celebration of and the response to Jesus. But the Eucharist was a local event enacted where humans lived and worked. It was a grass-roots experience. Humankind responded to God in the same way it lived, not as isolated atoms or as a massive collectivity but rather as a collection of small local communities, united in a common faith and a common goal. Global in its aims and vision, local in its daily life, federal in its organizational structure, the assembly offered the model by which human unity would eventually be restructured; that is, universal world vision, local autonomy, and organic structure linking the various local communities in a variegated but integrated unity.

Those who claimed to be the followers of Jesus have been considerably less than perfect in their fidelity to the insights that flowed from the Easter and Pentecost experiences. They have sometimes sacrificed world vision for rigid and defensive parochialism. They have sometimes allowed the degeneration of local communities, ceaselessly fighting among themselves and excommunicating (denying communion with) one another at the drop of a participle. They have sometimes taken away the legitimate independence of the local assembly and tried to reshape the Church on the model of a medieval monarchy, a Renaissance absolutist state, or a modern corporation. They have sometimes tried to impose an oppressive uniformity that denied the rightful variety of the human condition. They have often fallen victim to internal quarreling that occupied almost all of their time and energy. They have split apart in schism and heresy. They have even killed one another in the name of Jesus, who came only to reveal God's unifying love.

They even managed to do all these things at once. Indeed, except for killing one another, virtually all the other errors were present in New Testament times. Jesus, it would seem, could have used better judgment in selecting his followers—both then and now.

But acceptance of the message of Jesus, commitment to the Christ event, and the re-experience of Easter do not eliminate human freedom or change the basic structure of human personality. Jesus has provided us with the raw material for growth, but we must then grow, however slowly and painfully. The assembly of the followers of Jesus is made up of people who have committed themselves to try to respond to the Good News. They cannot commit themselves to perfection of response, at least not as long as they are weak and frail human beings. The Church is for humans, not angels. Its perfection is to be found, not in the virtue of its members, the wisdom of its leaders, or the elegance of its organizational structure; rather it is to be found in the person and the message of the One to whom it is attempting to respond.

If you can find a Church that is perfect, by all means join it; but realize that, when you do, it has ceased to be perfect.

If there is so much fragility, so much weakness, so much imperfection, so much corruption in the Church, then why have one at all? As a vision of a reconstituted humanity it certainly doesn't seem to have much to offer, does it?

The reason for a Church is simple enough: no man is an island. We cannot live by ourselves. We are responsible to others because of a basic human phenomenon: we need others to survive. The isolated loner is not more than human, he is less than human; he becomes a savage, an animal hunting in the jungle by himself. The human infant cannot survive without his parents, and he continues to need their help through the long years until he reaches physical maturity. We need others to listen to us, to learn from, to go to for help, to talk to, to take care of, to love and to be loved by. Our personality is formed, grows, and develops through our interaction with others. They heal us, protect us, challenge us, and comfort us. There is no worse punishment than to be cut off, ignored, sent into "Coventry" (as it was said in the English secondary schools of days gone by) or into solitary confinement. Religion, like every other form of human behavior, is necessarily social. We have a Church because we need help to respond to God's gift of himself, to the Good News that even our wildest dreams fall short of the truth. The Good News is too startling, too staggering, too demanding for us to be able to do anything about it by ourselves. We need the help of others.

The Church has all the faults of any human community in both its local and international forms. Still it is from the Church that we learn about Jesus. Our clergy, our teachers, our parents teach us who Jesus is and what he stands for by word and by example. If we are to experience the Christ event, if Easter is to be reenacted in the depths of our soul, then it can only happen in the Church. The Church is our link with the Christ event, and the link by which we will pass our experience of that event on to those who will come after us. The Church encourages, challenges, comforts, and in its best moments inspires us. Without it we could not be Christians.

Catholic Christianity believes that it is the adequate and comprehensive manifestation of the Church. It does not—after the Second Vatican Council at any rate—deny validity or reality to other Churches and ecclesiastical bodies. It admits its own faults and mistakes, and there have been many. But it still would contend that in the universality of its openness to the diversity of humankind, in its lineage that stretches back to apostolic times, in its internal unity, and in its commitment to both the basic goodness of human nature and the corporate nature of salvation, it can make a unique claim to be the Church of Jesus Christ. It prays for and works toward the unity of all Christians with respect and affection for its brothers and sisters in other Churches, while realizing that the time and mode of Christian unity, like the time and mode of the restoration of total human community, lie shrouded in the mists of the future, known only by the God who gave the gift and will eventually give its fulfillment.

Catholic Christians are under no illusion about the mistakes their Church has made, as well as the imperfections of which it and they have been guilty. The Church's claim to holiness rests, not on the personal virtue of its members, though many have been virtuous and some extremely so, but rather on the holiness of the Word it preaches, the Eucharist it celebrates, and the Lord it proclaims. Catholic Christians today, recalling the "catholic" enthusiasm of the early years, stand ready to learn from anyone—Protestant, Jew, nonbeliever—who has anything good to teach. The protective and defensive stand that may or may not have been appropriate during the battles of the Reformation and the Counter-Reformation eras has come to an end, and the assembly once again approaches the world with an open mind and an open heart. (Even though that openness has not, a mere decade after the end of the Second Vatican Council, yet permeated all the structures of the Church.)

Jesus certainly saw that there would emerge a community of those who had followed him and who would continue to preach his message. It would appear from our present understanding of the Scripture that he sketched the broad outlines of the principles that would animate the assembly of his followers; he left the details to those who would come after him. But he certainly realized that there would be leaders in his community, and he gave, by his own behavior as well as by his teaching, instructions on how those leaders should act.

The leader of a Christian community has two essential roles (and they are analogous to the role of a leader in any human community). On the one hand he must comfort and challenge, he must stir his followers out of their complacency and resist their parochialism. He must make them see the broader vision of the work they share with members of other communities, and he must encourage them when they are tired and weary, depressed and frustrated. He must incarnate in his own person the goals and ideals of the community and inspire and demand, as well as renew and invigorate, his followers by the life he leads and the person he is. He must be transparent so that his commitment radiates out to others.

On the other hand he also has a functional role. He is the "link person" that ties the local community (neighborhood, city, nation) to the next larger unit in the network of communities. He does that by speaking for the local church to the larger Church, and by speaking to the local church for the larger Church. He communicates to the other local churches the needs, insights, and talents of his own community. When he speaks at meetings of leaders he speaks for his community and not merely on his own initiative. But he also keeps his own community in touch with the needs and problems, opportunities and resources of other local churches and of the entire network. When he comes home from meetings he carries with him the obligation to speak for the whole of Christianity.

His leadership is necessarily one of service, for the Christian tradition knows no other kind of leadership. Linking, challenging, and comforting are all actions of service. They are to be carried out with the same affection and respect with which Jesus washed the feet of his followers. Listening to the voices within his community, he must discern those in whom the Spirit is speaking. Such discernment is also a form of service that must be carried on with great respect, tact, and affection.

For many centuries a certain authoritarian and dictatorial style has crept in from the world outside and has affected the behavior of some Church leaders. They have acted more like secular princes (which many of them were) rather than like servants of God's people. This style, which has lasted far too long, is beginning to wane in the aftermath of the Second Vatican Council. It hardly need be said that the defeat of an authoritarian and absolutist style of Church leadership is not yet complete.

But it is not only the leaders of the Church who must be servants. The Church itself is a servant Church; it must constantly strive to be a good servant. Christianity is committed to the ultimate fulfillment of the gift of human unity that Jesus came to bring from the heavenly Father. It believes that love means generous giving of oneself to others; it believes that the Good News of the Christ event is most effectively shown to others by the example of generous love that reflects the love God revealed to us in Jesus. It must therefore manifest loving service in its own internal relationships, in its corporate (both local and collective) behavior toward the world outside, and in the concern that its members manifest in struggling against human misery. Social concern is not a substitute for religious commitment but is an essential consequence of it.

So, to the question of whether humankind can find unity, the mystery of the Church says that it can, but only when the insight of fellow feeling is sufficiently strong so that loving service of the stranger who is our brother begins to transform social structures. As the community of those who believe in such love, the Church is, in principle, and should be in fact, the model and the paradigm for the new humanity.

It is surely not much of a model or a paradigm now, but if

such is the fault of the Church, the blame lies not with its vision or its word or its sacraments. The blame lies with its members. with us.

THEOLOGICAL AND ORGANIZATIONAL NOTES

1. Many of the elements of Catholic Christianity as we now find it are historical developments. The Roman Curia, the College of Cardinals, the Code of Canon Law, ecclesiastical celibacy, the ceremony of the papacy, for examples, are no more part of the essence of Catholic Christianity than was the Latin Mass. They could be dropped tomorrow and the Church would still be the Church. The critical question that must be asked about all these historical developments is whether they are conducive to the effectiveness of the Church's mission today. The answer to that question is not always easy to find, and people of good will can disagree about it. But while these developments are important, they are not essential and should not obscure the basic purpose of the Church.

2. It is often said that the Church is not a democracy. To the extent that such a statement has any meaning at all, one could reply by saying that it is not a monarchy either. The Church is indeed a human institution, and as such, it is roughly comparable with other human institutions; but it is not a government, and analogies with governmental forms become inappropriate when pushed too far.

There were far more democratic procedures in the early and medieval Church than there were in the modern era. Bishops (including the Bishop of Rome, for example) were elected by the clergy and people of their own dioceses. Abbots in monasteries are still elected by their monks. Heads of religious communities are frequently still elected by members of the community—

particularly if the communities are medieval in origin. Two popes in late antiquity argued that any other method of selection of the local Church leader was seriously sinful. Pope Leo I flatly laid down the rule that "he who presides over all ought to be chosen by all." John Carroll, the first American bishop, insisted that he would not serve if he were not elected by the priests of the country, because, he argued, no other manner of election would be appropriate in America. There is considerable evidence that the Church is moving toward a drastic redemocratization of its procedures with such institutions as national conferences of bishops, diocesan pastoral councils, and parish councils. For some this change is moving too slowly, for others too rapidly. Persons of good will can disagree about its wisdom; there are advantages and disadvantages, as the experience of our more democratically organized Protestant brothers and sisters makes clear. The point, however, is that there is nothing in the essential nature of the Church that precludes such change.

3. Even many ecumenical Protestant scholars will admit the need for a chief bishop in Christianity, a man who is the incarnation of and the spokesman for the Church. They will disagree with Catholics about the nature and scope of such a leader's authority, though more recently the disagreement seems to be less on the principle of such leadership and more on the way it has been exercised in recent centuries. There are, many Protestants would say, modalities of the exercise of papal authority that would be both true to Catholic doctrine and acceptable to Protestant practice.

No matter how these theological and organizational problems will be resolved, Catholic Christianity is committed to two points about the papacy. (1) The pope is the presiding bishop of the Church and the unique and special leader who, under God's guidance, presides over the whole Church; and (2) the popes, as inept and even evil as some may have been, had the power, by virtue of that divine guidance, to prevent the Church from the kind of mistake that would lead it to stray completely from the message and thus destroy itself. The importance of papal leadership and the immense impact of that leadership on the whole of humankind was especially evident in the years of Pope John XXIII. If there were more popes with such skills, the theoretical questions about authority, primacy, and infallibility—while still knotty and important—might be solved with relatively less difficulty than most of us would have thought.

Historical and Doctrinal Note

There has developed a considerable amount of agreement between Protestants and Catholics in ecumenical dialogue on the subject of the Papacy. Both sides now agree on the preeminent role of Peter in the early Church, and the need in the Church at all times of a "Petrine function"—a role in the universal Church that promotes the unity and cooperation of all local churches. Many Protestants are willing to admit the ancient claim of the Church of Rome to fulfill in predominant measure that function. Catholics, on the other hand, argue that the role of Rome in the "Petrine function" pertains to "things of God" in the Church— and hence can be said to be of divine origin emerged very slowly in the early centuries and has been exercised in many different styles down through the years. Furthermore, Catholics in the dialogue also say that documents and doctrines about the role of the Pope, while certainly true, will be misunderstood unless they are studied in the historical context in which they were produced. Hence, one must not approach a doctrine about the Papacy with the concerns and interests of the present time, but rather with the concerns and interests of the men who wrote the documents laying out the doctrines. Finally, Catholics also would say that it would be a mistake for both sides to consider that the Papal administrative style of any given time (including the present) is part of the essence of the Papal role.

This emerging consensus does not solve all remaining problems, but it has taken the discussion far beyond the arguments that occupied so much time and energy not so long ago.

SOCIAL THEORY NOTE

Catholic social theory, reflecting on Catholic understanding of the revelations about the nature of human nature in the Christ event, takes a more benign view of human society than do many other social theories. It does not think of society as an oppressive agency that forces cooperation on uncooperative and aggressive individuals. Instead, it believes that society is the actual result of the social nature of humankind, and that the dense and intimate network of social relationships of each human exists, not to oppress the individual but to facilitate his or her growth. When oppression does occur (which is not infrequently), Catholic Christianity believes that it is the result of an abuse of social power and not its natural exercise. Because of this respect for the web of human relationships, particularly the most intimate and local ones, Catholic social theory is skeptical of attempts to change society through drastic, once-and-for-all techniques; and it is generally committed to organic growth that, instead of wiping the social slate clean, moves individuals and communities forward from where they are. Furthermore, its realization of the crucial importance of the local church community leads Catholic social theory to insist on the principle of subsidiarity, the idea that nothing should be done by larger and more centralized agencies that can be done equally well by smaller and more local groups. Needless to say, the Church has not always followed this principle itself in regulating and organizing its own life.

SOCIAL ACTION NOTE

Catholicism does not believe that specific solutions to concrete social and economic problems can be derived from the Gospel. Individual Christians and groups of Christians can and must take stands on specific issues in light of how they see the Gospel applying to specific situations, but they must not claim unique validity for their application of principles to practice. Even Church leaders may take stands on specific issues (though they ought to be reluctant to do so unless they are adequately informed), but they should clearly distinguish their own private positions from the teachings of the Gospel. Finally, the Church as an organization may commit itself to one side or the other in some particularly crucial conflict, but it should do so with the full awareness that it may well be making a mistake, and that its political and social stand is much more contingent than the Gospel it preaches. What makes Christian social action unique is not so much the specific solutions it offers (though it will incline toward maximizing personal freedom and local initiative when it is being true to its own best insights) but the style with which it is exercised. The Christian acts with patience, serenity, flexibility, refusal to hate, eagerness to reconcile, and implacable perseverance no matter how many defeats and frustrations he suffers.

Chapter Nine

THE MYSTERY OF BAPTISM

Can we live in harmony with nature?

(Is there any way to be saved without baptism?)

W E ARE AT ODDS WITH OUR NATURAL ENVIRONMENT. WE breathe its air, we eat of its foods and flocks, we drink its water. Yet in the last hundred and fifty years we have shamefully exploited it (whether we live in capitalist or socialist countries). We pollute the air, we strip the land, we poison the water. We are responsible for the environment because, unlike other creatures, we are not preprogrammed in its use. We must exercise free choice in adjusting ourselves to the material world of which we are a part. Since we have intelligence, it is not permitted to us merely to accept the environment as it is. The material world can adapt a multitude of different forms, some much more conducive to a free human life than others. Virtually no one will think that the elimination of cholera from our lake and river waters is a mistake, and only a few will argue that the prairies should not have been turned into the richest crop-producing land the world has ever known. (It is another question whether some prairie land should have been preserved in its natural state.)

But it is one thing to say that humans have the power to

alter and reshape the environment to make it more rational and benign, and it is quite another to assume that humankind is the lord of the world and can do with it whatever it wants. Yet this is the way we have lived for several centuries. We have used the world (and that is proper—the iron ore in the Mesabi range wasn't doing anyone any good under the ground), but we have not used it with respect or reverence. Now the environment is fighting back with broken natural cycles turning destructive and threatening the humans who broke them.

This misuse of the material world and its vengeance upon us is but one manifestation of the ambiguity humankind has felt about the world in which it finds itself. For that world is both benign and destructive. It provides us with our food, drink, clothing, housing; but it also destroys. Floods, hurricanes, cyclones, typhoons, tornados, droughts, winter snow and ice, blight, disease, predatory animals, erosion—all have suggested to humankind that there is disorder in the world just as there is disorder in human personality. The world is our friend, but it is also our enemy.

Worse still, the world seems to imprison us. We aspire to be everywhere, to see everything, to do all that there is to do, to have all that there is to have; but we are still enmeshed in the threads of time and place. The demands of our body are insistent; they slow us down, burden us, weary us: For a long time many humans felt that the body was a prison in which the human spirit was temporarily captured, and that the purpose of human life was to progressively break free of the chains and bars of such a prison. In the West such a theory has not been explicitly propounded in recent times except by the increasingly numerous advocates of Eastern religious beliefs and practices. We often live as though we have forgotten that we have bodies that tie us irrevocably to the natural process in which they (and hence we) are immersed. Examples are the intellectual who thinks rational and scientific analysis is the only way to truth, and the self-described Christian who is convinced the body is dirty and so hangs on to the "spirituality" of the soul; both share a resentment toward the fact that we are animal, that we are, as one writer has said, a "spirit who must excrete."

Water is the primal element. (We know now, of course, that it is not an element at all but is made up of two more basic elements.) It is the matrix in which all else exists. The continents "float" on the oceans, our bodies are mostly water; it is essential for our life. Yet it is terribly destructive, too, wiping out fields, flocks, towns, and people. Water is the source of both life and death. As the primal element of the world in which we live, water has all the ambiguities of the rest of the environment in a quintessential way. It brings life, it causes destruction, it imprisons us because of our thirst for it and because of the immense barriers it creates to our freedom of movement.

We know the fear of trying to drive a car at night in a blinding rainstorm or on a frozen and slippery road. We know the sheer terror of being threatened by a combination of wind and water that whips waves to a frenzy; we have seen wreckage caused by flood, hurricane, tidal wave, and tornado; we have read how too much rain or not enough can reduce the summer's harvest, cause a world food shortage, and force up the price of food; we experience the frustration when bad weather ruins a holiday.

Yet we know the pleasure of a cold drink when we are thirsty, the joy of diving into a lake or pool on a hot summer's day, the comfort of a warm bath or a brisk shower when we are tense and tired. We know the relief of a rainstorm that ends a long hot spell, and the beauty of snowflakes gently covering the brown and barren earth. As the primal element in our world, the primary matrix of our life, water participates in the fundamental ambiguity of life. It brings both life and death. Which part of its revelation is most essential? Which is a better hint of an explanation of the meaning of our existence? As Jews, the early followers of Jesus had no doubt that the environment was good. Yahweh had made it and that was that. Yet their law prohibited many material things, often for reasons that were socially functional when the laws were created—meat that was easily spoiled and poisoned, for example. But many of the sects among them were obsessed with the fear that they might be rendered "impure" by the corruption of the world around them. Hence these sectaries spent considerable amounts of time in ritual hand-washings and baths. Furthermore, Jews were suspicious of the pagan tendency to worship the forces of nature superstitiously (despite the vestiges of nature rites in their own religion). Finally, the Jewish intellectuals of their time—particularly outside of Palestine— could not help but be influenced by Platonic philosophy and its religious descendent, Gnosticism, both of which were strongly antimaterial and antibody.

But in the Christ event at Easter the followers of Jesus learned that the material world was saved too. God gave his supreme gift of himself, his ultimate revelation of himself, not in the form of a Gnostic angel but in the form of a man who eats, drinks, grows weary, and falls asleep like all other men. God had entered the cosmos, not as pure spirit but as very much part of the material world. Therefore, that world was holy. The body of Jesus shared in the resurrection, and that settled the matter once and for all. The world was good. It was both the object and the means of salvation. It was the recipient of grace. It revealed God's gift to us. Indeed it was part of the gift. The world is grace.

In the first flush of their enthusiasm, the early Christians embraced the material world just as they embraced human culture. Pagan rituals, which had been excluded from Judaism for fear they would corrupt the faith of the people, were quickly transformed, purified with a Christian interpretation, and made part of the life of the people.

So water, the primal element, once again became sacred. Ritual purifications had always been part of the Jewish religion. The wandering preachers of the time, John the Baptist and Jesus himself, apparently, had baptized their followers as a sign of their repentance (borrowing the practice, we think, from the Dead Sea sectaries—or perhaps both groups had borrowed from an older tradition about which we know very little). So it was perfectly natural for the followers of Jesus to begin to use baptism as a rite of initiating a person into the community of Christians. But the assembly of the disciples of Jesus had far more to proclaim than the need for personal transformation. It viewed the basic Good News to be the Word that, in Jesus, God had revealed himself as willing the triumph of life over death. So, very early, baptism became a ceremony much richer in its implications than a simple ritual of moral transformation. It came to stand for an introduction into a community of life, a fellowship of grace.

With that interpretation, baptism became one more of the mysteries that revealed the meaning of the Christ event. All the rich water symbolism of the nature religions (based in turn, it would seem, on the very structure of the human unconscious, as it is revealed to us in dreams and fantasies) and of the Hebrew religion itself were now available to explain the meaning of baptism and what it told us about the Christ event. Very early we find St. Paul insisting on baptism as a symbol of life and death, a burial with Jesus as a prelude and a cause of a resurrection with him. (And in the practice of baptism by immersion—the only one known in the early Church—one was quite literally buried in water.) Just as the wandering Hebrews were reconciled into a people and liberated from the slavery of Egypt in the Exodus event of passing through the waters of the Red Sea, so Christians become a unified and reconciled people by passing, under the leadership of Jesus, the new Moses, through the life-giving waters of baptism. The sacred waters of the old pagan religions became now the gracious (grace-giving) waters of Christianity, bringing death to the old man and life to the new in Christ Jesus.

Baptism, then, like the Eucharist, became the means by which the Christ event would be reenacted, by which the Easter experience would be continued in time and space. It was an initiation rite, of course, but it was one that showed that by joining the assembly one experienced a death and resurrection event, one was dying with Jesus so that one might rise with him to a fresh new life.

The ambiguity of water was no more denied than was the ambiguity of the physical world and the ambiguity of human life. But in the light of the Christ event, water was seen as grace, as a revelation. Life and death were combined in water, but life was stronger, and even the death dimension of water was a prelude to and a cause of life. The joys and the pleasures of water were the hints of an explanation, not only about the meaning of water but about the meaning of life.

The link between baptism and the Easter experience was emphasized by the fact that for many centuries baptism (normally at least) took place only as part of the Easter vigil service. The new Christians would die with Christ at the same time he died and they would rise with him very early in the morning on the first day of the week. We continue even today the custom of blessing the baptismal waters and renewing our baptismal commitments at Eastertime.

The early Christians also saw water as the great bond that linked humans together. The baptismal waters united humans and God the way the marriage act united man and wife. The rich sexual symbolism of water was obvious to those Roman Christians who appropriated the pagan spring fertility rite of the lighted candle (the male organ) and the waters (womb), using it for the blessing of the baptismal waters. In the Easter event, God is united with his people, Christ is united with his bride the Church, and the newly baptized Christian is the offspring of this union.

Other human signs began to receive special gracious meanings: oil (anointing and dedication to a work), human leadership, healing of sickness, reconciliation, and marriage. These were now thought of as sacraments, as special and efficacious signs of God's grace at work. Through oil, fire, water, bread, and wine; through the friendship of others; and through the attractive body of a human of the opposite sex, God was at work in the world. He was giving himself to us as a continuation of the gift in Jesus. Indeed, these quite ordinary and mundane things were now seen as a continuation of the Christ event. In the sacraments, and indeed in the sacramental signs themselves, the Easter experience became present to us once again.

But these various signs are able to be sacraments, are able to convey grace to us, precisely because all material elements are gracious. All things reveal God's goodness to us if we know how to look for it. The whole world is a sacrament, a revelation of graciousness. In the Christian view of things the natural powers—water, fire, air, fertility—are not sacred in themselves but rather in what they reveal. The Christian might more appropriately speak of them as gracious instead of sacred. They reveal goodness because they participate in goodness, or, to become metaphysical for a moment, they reveal being because they share in Being.

Grace, then, lurks everywhere—in brickyards and back alleys, in the snow and the wind, in the sun and the stars, in the waters and the fire, in the tiny flower, and in the volcano. It is in the branches of trees, in weeds, in the chirping of birds, as well as in the roar of an elevated train, and in the desirable body of another. The environment is a sacrament, and to ruthlessly exploit it is a sacrilege. The world is a chalice of grace, and to treat it with disrespect is blasphemy. The world is grace, and not to appreciate it is ingratitude.

But the world is not a passive sacrament; the environment does not stand idly by waiting for us to perceive its graciousness. The Holy Spirit, who, after the Christ event, began to take over as the Lord of the world, is actively pursuing us with a world that commands our attention with its splendors and invites our admiration with its beauty.

And grace is not merely lurking around the corner waiting for us; it is chasing us madly down the street.

Chapter Ten

THE MYSTERY OF MARY THE MOTHER OF JESUS

Can we find our sexual identity?
(Is Mary truly the mother of God?)

S EX BAFFLES US. IT ALWAYS HAS. IT IS THE MOST PLEASURA-ble of human physical activities but also the most confusing. It takes very little to awaken sexual desire but it is extremely difficult to sustain a long sexual relationship. Sex offers us the most rewarding of human intimacies but the demands that such intimacy places upon our personality are so insistent that frequently the intimacy dissolves or settles down to mutual coexistence. We cannot couple without personal involvement as animals do; such sexual activity may temporarily lower physical tension but it does not satisfy the interpersonal needs and emotions which we can exclude from our sex life only with very great difficulty. Since we are meaning-seeking creatures, we must find meaning in our sexuality.

There has been, it is alleged, a sexual revolution. We are told that we live in a permissive society. Surely there is more talk about sex than there was a hundred years ago and more erotic materials readily available to us than to our parents. Whether we are any more permissive than people were in other periods of history may be questioned, but such is hardly the point. Through the insights of depth psychology we understand intellectually a good deal more about the role of sexuality in personality development and the dynamics of sexual attraction than did our parents. We are also far more aware than most of our ancestors were of the rights and privileges of women.

It does not follow, however, that we are any less afraid of our sexuality or that we enjoy it more. Some observers report that our younger generation, supposedly free from sexual hang-ups, is retreating from love because of fear of personal involvement. Divorces are increasing. Too many first marriages end in divorce, and even more second marriages fall prey to the same fate. Experts freely predict the end of the institution of marriage. But the alternatives do not seem inviting to most people; frequently they turn out to be merely fashionably rationalized exploitation—usually of women. So far humankind has found no more efficient or satisfying way of arranging most of its sexual relationships other than the relatively permanent commitment of a man and a woman to each other, with varying kinds of exclusivity involved in the commitment. There are other forms of heterosexual activity, of course, but they account for a relatively small amount of the total acts of intercourse performed each night, and there is no real reason to think the proportion has gone up in our time. Marriages may end more easily today than they did in the past, but that simply means there will be, for weal or woe, more marriages.

The condition of marriage today, or anytime, is a revealing symptom of our problems with sexuality. In principle, marriage *is* more than merely an effective and convenient way of satisfying passion and rearing children. It is supposed to be the opportunity *par excellence* for combining physical pleasure with interpersonal communion. It is supposed to be the context of the strongest possible human love. Most people expect their principal life satisfaction and self-fulfillment to come from their marriage relationship. Hardly anyone enters a marriage any more without at least modest expectations for happiness. Yet many marriages turn into disasters, others are less than rewarding, and even the best are frequently plagued by strain and tension. Sex drives us toward another person; it often opens up our spirit as well as our body to embrace the other in deep and rich human love. Yet the very intimacy into which our sexual passion forces us produces friction and conflict. The life space of the marriage bed and the family house or apartment seems too confined for two humans to occupy for very long without getting on each other's nerves. We are drawn together by a mixture of physical hunger and emotional attraction—which can serve as a good beginning for love. But the emotional attraction all too easily turns into repulsion, and if the hunger does not diminish, its satisfaction often loses much of the reward it once seemed to promise.

How come?

The answer is that sex scares us. No matter how practiced or sophisticated or nonchalant we may try to be, we are afraid of the sexual encounter. Some of this fear is based on childhood problems and bad sexual education, but we are kidding ourselves if we think the basic cause of sexual fear does not go much deeper in the personality. We are afraid of the other person. He or she is different from us biologically, psychologically, or humanly. We do not understand him, we cannot predict his behavior, we have only the dimmest notion of his needs and expectations. He will see us in our most defenseless and vulnerable psychological and physiological state; he will be evaluating our body, our personhood, our performance in an area in which we are very unsure. He has access to our body and our emotions that we are very reluctant to grant. He can bring us great affection and pleasure, but he can also reject us, ridicule us, humiliate us, and torment us. We humans are very careful indeed about whom we give power over our intimate self; yet our sexuality forces us to turn over that which is most intimate in us to someone who often seems almost a total stranger.

Furthermore we have our sex under rather poor control; it forces us to do things that are undignified and that we would be ashamed to have others witness. Worse still, it pushes us into relationships of which we are afraid. Frequently it leads us to actions which are clearly stupid and irrational, and for which we feel guilty. Bad enough that it is so powerful a force, but, worse still, we control it so poorly.

Small wonder that so many philosophies thought sex evil. If humankind is a spirit trapped in a body, the most obvious and most animal part of the cage is sex. Small wonder, too, that so many religions are darkly suspicious of sex; it surely interferes with reflection and contemplation. The early nature religions believed sex was sacred; anything that powerful had to pertain to "the Other." In addition, fertility of animal and plant and human was necessary for the perpetuation of the tribe. But it was not clear to the nature religions whether the sacred power of sexuality was benign. Some of the darkest, wildest, and most evil of the nature deities were devouring goddesses who linked sexuality, birth, and death in most awful ("awe-full") ways.

Yet we know that sex can be a revelatory experience. There are times when it hints to us very powerfully indeed that the Something Else out there must be very gracious to have thought up such an interesting and rewarding way to keep the species going. For some people sex is the trigger for mystical ecstatic experiences. The majority of us do not go from orgasm to mystical ecstasy (and people who do say that the mystical interlude is specifically different and far more spectacular than orgasm), but we do know that sex has the power to turn us on. It is a dull, gloomy, miserable day; then an attractive person of the opposite sex crosses our line of vision. We may not speak, we may never see each other again, but it is as though a flash of light has broken through the darkness. Here is beauty, here is elegance, here is pleasure. At the end of a frustrating, battering day, when the world seems mean and harsh and unfeeling, it is important for most people to discover in the arms of the beloved that there is still tenderness and affection on the earth, that we are still lovable (and capable of loving), that in a rhythm of mutual giving and receiving we can give, that which is best in us and receive the best of the other in return. In such moments we know that there is goodness in the human condition, that there is graciousness in the universe.

Christianity came into being at a rather interesting time in the history of human sexuality. The Hebrews had a realistic and matter-of-fact approach to sex. Marriage, intercourse, and children were part of human life, they were gifts from Yahweh and they were meant to be used. They were not particularly given to romantic ideas—although, as the Song of Songs shows, they were by no means incapable of powerful romantic emotions. In such writings as Osee, Jeremias, and Ezekiel, the Hebrews united imagery from romantic love or portray the hunger of God for his people. The later prophet, Zephaniah, even described Israel as a "corporate person" (A favorite Old Testament literary form in which a person stands for the whole community). The people were the "virgin daughter of Sion" for whom Yahweh longed as the bridegroom for a bride.

Generally the Jews were very skeptical of mixing sexuality with their worship. Yahweh had to contend with the fertility cults of Canaan for supremacy in the land, and the victory over the cults of the "high places" (apparently the hilltops where the rituals occurred) was not an easy one. Israel had a horror of mixing "filth" with its devotion to Yahweh. So it abhorred the frequently debasing fertility rites that were so much a part of the folk religion of the Roman Empire at the time of Jesus.

A very different strain of thought, however, was going on in the Greek culture. People took care of their sexual needs, of course, but convinced as they were that humankind was spirit, the philosophers regretted that bodily demands and social responsibilities forced them to engage in such lowly behavior. Sex was low, base, and foul; and to the minds of some, relationships with one's own sex (usually male) were superior to heterosexuality, since friendship was possible with other men but scarcely so with such "second-rate" creatures as women, who were "incapable of philosophizing." This contempt for sex dominated the intellectual milieu into which Christianity moved when it left Palestine. It was inevitable that Christianity would be tainted by it if it was to use neoplatonic philosophy to explain itself to the pagan world.

So Christianity arrived on the scene in an environment created by the realism of the Jews—which was complicated by images of romantic love and the frequently vile superstitions of the pagan folk religion that was part of the Jewish tradition—and the horror of sex that was beginning to dominate the philosophical view of human nature. What happened is still astonishing.

The Christ event revealed that grace is in the world. Everything was defined for salvation. God gave himself to us and all things were to be renewed through and in Christ. The world was starting all over again. In the exuberance of the Easter experience there was no room for the gloom of pessimistic paganism with its contempt for the human body. Was it not a body that hung on the cross and rose from the dead? How could the body be evil?

By the time of St. Paul (and hence very early—even before the Gospels had been written down) the marriage image of the Old Testament had been taken over and put to use to describe the Easter experience. The gift of God to us in Jesus and our gift in response was like the exchange of gifts between husband and wife (a fact that was not completely forgotten through all the years of antisexual neoplatonism). Marriage was a sacrament (in the nontheological sense of being a revelation of a secret) of the passionate love of God for us.

Then two currents of very early Christian reflection began to drift together. The assembly of the followers of Jesus began to be thought of as the new Israel, the new People of God. Jesus was described as the new Adam who gave humankind a fresh start. If the Church was Israel, then there was a need for a corporate personality that could stand for the Church the way the Daughter of Zion in the late prophetic literature stood for the people. Yahweh longed for his people as a husband does for his bride. If Jesus was the new Adam, it seemed appropriate for there to be a new Eve. For reasons we do not know (though they may very well have something to do with the qualities of the historical person herself) the early Christians assigned this role to Mary the mother of Jesus. So by the time the Gospels were written, we have in the infancy stories a "protomariology" in which the mother of Jesus is already playing the corporate role as the new Daughter of Zion. She has already begun to represent the Church, and at the same time, particularly in the virginal conception account, she is being assigned a role as the new Eve, the mother of a new humanity. In St. John's Gospel we have a more elaborately developed mariology in both the Cana and the crucifixion scenes, where Mary is quite explicitly identified with the Church.

This is still a corporate mariology. Mary is present, not so much as an individual person but as someone who stands for the whole Church. But within a hundred years, a personal mariology also developed. As part of the exuberant enthusiasm of the early Christians, Mary replaced the mother goddesses of the pagan world. In theory she was not a goddess, but she played a role for Christianity that was functionally similar to those that the female deities had played in antiquity: she reflected the feminine aspect of God.

No one could possibly have expected such a development. The Hebrew religion abhorred the goddesses. Yahweh was beyond sexuality (and his pre-Sinai consort, Shekenna, had been reduced to nothing more than the glory of his presence). But in its extraordinary openness and self-confidence, Christianity was less worried about corruption. If there was truth and goodness and beauty in the notion of a feminine deity, Christianity would take over the idea and integrate it into its own world view. If sexual union was revelatory, then feminine humanity, as well as masculine humanity, could reveal God to us, and Mary was God's self-revelation through femininity in its perfection. And thus there came to the Western world what may well be the most powerful cultural symbol it has known for the last two thousand years.

One of humankind's earliest insights into the nature of God was that those attributes that constitute both masculine and feminine perfection are intermingled and combined in the deity. Some of the most ancient gods were androgynous. They had both masculine and feminine characteristics that were later to be separated. Whatever it that was "out there" was strong, direct, and aggressive like a brave hunter or a resourceful tracker or a hardworking farmer. But it was also gentle, tender, and compassionate like a mother nursing a child, a young woman inspiring a warrior as he went into battle, a wife gently caring for her husband by the campfire at the end of a dangerous hunt, or even an older woman holding in her arms the body of her dying son, fatally wounded in battle or the hunt.

We know from primitive art that the feminine deity was a *Madonna* (the mother who gave life and who presided over the fertility of the earth), a *Virgo* (the beautiful but untouchable inspiration), a *sponsa* (the pleasure-giving spouse), and a *pieta* (the goddess of death, the earth receiving back in death that which it once gave to life). All these manifestations of the femininity of God were easily corruptible, but they revealed that God the active creator is also God the tender lover. Once Christianity took the critical step of permitting a personal mariology, it was natural that Mary be depicted in each of these roles. Michelangelo's *Madonna of the Barrelbead and Pieta* sum it all up visually; and long before the history of religions sorted out the various roles of the mother goddess, Gerard Manley Hopkins caught it in "The May Magnificat."

May is Mary's month, and I
Muse at that and wonder why:
Her feasts follow reason,
Dated due to season—

Candlemas, Lady Day;
But the Lady Month, May,
Why fasten that upon her,
With a feasting in her honour?

Is it only its being brighter
Than the most are must delight her?
Is it opportunest
And flowers finds soonest?

Ask of her, the mighty mother:
Her reply puts this other
Question: What is Spring?—
Growth in every thing—

Flesh and fleece, fur and feather,
Grass and greenworld all together;
Star-eyed strawberry-breasted
Throstle above her nested

Cluster of bugle blue eggs thin
Forms and warms the life within;
And bird and blossom swell
In sod or sheath or shell.

All things rising, all things sizing
Mary sees, sympathising
With that world of good,
Nature's motherhood.

Their magnifying of each its kind
With delight calls to mind
How she did in her stored
Magnify the Lord.

Well but there was more than this:
Spring's universal bliss
Much, had much to say
To offering Mary May.

When drops-of-blood-and-foam-dapple
Bloom lights the orchard-apple
And thicket and thorp are merry
With silver-surfed cherry

And azuring-over greybell makes
Wood banks and brakes wash wet like lakes
And magic cuckoo call
Caps, clear, and clinches all

This ecstasy all through mothering earth
Tells Mary her mirth till Christ's birth
To remember and exultation
In God who was her salvation.

"The May Magnificat"
Gerard Manley Hopkins (1844–1889)

Influenced by neoplatonism, Christian theology may have shrunk from facing the femininity of Mary. Fortunately, artists like Michelangelo and poets like Hopkins knew better.

So the mystery of Mary the mother of Jesus crystallizes the Christian faith that sexuality is not only good but also revelatory, and Christianizes the ancient human faith that both masculine and feminine must be combined in whatever is "out there." The idea that Mary represents and reveals to us the tenderness of God need have nothing to do with rigid definitions of masculine and feminine roles or personality traits. On the contrary, in the revelation that God is androgynous we are liberated from rigidity and permitted to develop the multifaceted dimensions of our own personalities; and whether we are man or woman, we are free to combine aggressiveness with tenderness, courage with gentleness, competitiveness with sympathy, the ordering of life with the giving of life. Certain kinds of mariology may have become linked with an "eternal feminine" ideology that seems to some to restrict women to permanent second-class positions. But there is no such ideology at the core of the mystery of Mary the mother of Jesus. She reveals to us only that God is our loving mother as well as our powerful father.

Intellectually and historically it may be a long way around from the protomariology of the infancy stories to our own agonizing over sexual identity; psychologically, however, it is but a quick leap. If God is not only our powerful father but also our loving mother, then it is safe to risk oneself in sexual encounter, for in the long run we cannot get hurt. If God gave himself totally to us in the Christ event, we can give ourselves totally to our partner, not only in the marriage bed but also in the common life. If the sexual union is a sacrament of the Christ event, then we need not fear its terrors and can more readily give ourselves over to its pleasures. Some Christians may have tried to desexualize Mary (though Christian art and literature has cancelled this effort), but she still represents the powerful and tender flow of the life forces at work in the world, and guarantees that we can give ourselves over to these forces with joy and confidence. The mystery of Mary the mother of Jesus does not promise that strains, frictions, and conflicts will be eliminated from our intimate relationships; but she does promise us the resources we need to learn from our mistakes, to rise up from our failures, and to confidently and joyously begin again—just as the human race began again with the birth of her son Jesus.

In rural Poland there used to be a custom that the young bride and groom would rise from the bed after consummating their marriage and recite the Magnificat (the prayer of Mary) together in gratitude to Mary for the joys of their union. It was imagined that Mary had been present with them in their first act of love, guarding and protecting them. The marriage chamber was hardly the place where the sexless piety of the official mariological devotions would have wanted Mary the mother of Jesus to be. But the shrewd peasant mind knew better. The young couple needed special help and protection at such a moment of both terror and happiness. To whom else would they turn besides God our loving mother, as represented to us by Mary the mother of Jesus?

THEOLOGICAL NOTES

1. The various marian titles can all be subsumed under four: mother, bride, spouse, and virgin. The central historical basis for the titles, and for the mariological symbols and theology from which they come, is the fact that Jesus was born of a human mother, Mary. Most Christians have called Mary the mother of God because of an ancient theological custom called the "communication of idioms," which was based on the philosophical terminology used in the third- and fourth-century controversies over Jesus. Jesus was described in these terms as having both a

divine and human nature but being only a divine person. Whatever was said of the human nature could also by this custom be predicated of the person. Thus as the mother of the man Jesus (the human nature), Mary could be said to be the mother of God. Obviously, in the strict sense of the word, God does not have a mother, and the misunderstanding of the custom of speech has needlessly offended and confused people. In the terminology we are using in this catechism it could be said that Mary is the mother of God because she is the mother of the man with whom God is most completely united and in whom He most totally discloses himself to us. Further clarification must await progress in current attempts to restate the nature of the union of "man like us" and "something more than human" in modern philosophical categories.

2. There is some controversy today over the virginal conception of Jesus. It is an important point, though it should not distract us from the still more important question of belief in the revelation of Jesus. How he came into the world is far less important than why. Clearly the authors of the infancy narratives are emphasizing a new beginning for humankind in Jesus, who, like Adam, is depicted as not having an earthly father. Whether this is a theological reflection only or a reflection combined with a historical claim is at present a matter of hot debate among Scripture scholars. Nor is it a solution to the debate to say that a virginal conception is "scientifically impossible." Having created the universe, God can choose any way he wants to re-create it. Furthermore, the argument that the virginal conception is "anti-sex" merely indicates that some misguided Christians have used it as part of their own antisex misunderstanding of Christianity. The burden of the New Testament message leaves no doubt that sexuality, like all other good things of this world, was liberated and reconciled in the Christ event. On the basis of the present scholarly analysis of the infancy stories, it can be said that while

they are obviously theological in intent, the virginal conception tradition is Palestinian (not Greek, as some had thought), very ancient, unlike any other story of divine incarnations in its tact and simplicity, and quite foreign to the Hebrew's religious tradition. If it were merely theological "fiction," it is hard to understand where the story came from or how it developed.

HISTORICAL NOTE

The early Church admitted women as full-fledged participants in the community. St. Paul sees no distinction between male or female in Christ Jesus. The Mary symbol went a long way toward improving the degraded position of women in pagan society. Women had great power in the medieval Church, presiding over vast lands and, as in the case of the Irish St. Brigid, even ruling monasteries of men as well. While there is no documented case of the ordination of women to the priesthood, it is now certain that the women deaconesses were considered to be in sacred orders, and that the women heads of monastic communities had certain powers that bishops possessed (such as giving "faculties" to hear confession and assigning priests to parishes). Such powers were exercised even into the nineteenth century. In many ways the Church has been and still is backward in extending full rights to women. On the other hand, particularly in the United States, women have had more "check-signing" power in the Church than in any other human organization. Today many women are working as leaders in parishes and in diocesan offices.

Chapter Eleven

THE MYSTERY OF HEAVEN

Why is life not fair?

(After death what happens to the good and evil?)

Lᴵꜰᴇ ɪꜱ ɴᴏᴛ ꜰᴀɪʀ. Iᴛ ɪꜱ ɴᴏᴛ ᴍᴇʀᴇʟʏ ᴛʜᴀᴛ ᴛʜᴇ ɪɴɴᴏᴄᴇɴᴛ suffer (so, too, do the good) and that the evil flourish. Everyone may be born equal in their moral dignity, but we are born very unequal in our physiological endowments, our social background, the energy our parents invest in us, our intellectual talents, and our capacity for hard work. It does not seem fair that one young man is the best quarterback in the league and another young man no good at sports at all. It is not fair that some young people can go abroad to the finest schools and that others must go to schools that are little more than places of temporary custody. It is not fair that some have high IQs and get high scores in tests while others have to work hard just to pass. It is not fair that some go to Harvard and others to junior colleges. It is not fair that some are beautiful and others plain. It is not fair that some own the newest Rolls or Mercedes while others drive old beaters. It is not fair that some live long and others die young. Or that some live relatively free from illness while others are plagued by chronic pain and disease.

It is from the unfairness of things that both envy, ideology, and demagoguery come. We hate the beautiful woman, the superlative athlete, or the rich young person. We want what they have; it is not fair that they should have so much and we so little. We spin out visions of a society in which there would be complete equality, not just of opportunity but of outcome, even if it means penalizing the talented, the innovative, the creative. (Of course such ideologists leave room for some inequality in such societies; there certainly would be some inequality of power since someone (they) would have to run the society.) We rally voters around our cause with the battle cry "Soak the rich and spread it out thin!"

But even those of us who can resign ourselves to the unfairness of the distribution of natural talents and, even worse, the unfairness of the distribution of health and happiness in this life are affronted by the success of those who appear to be evil. The leaders of the crime syndicates, business operators with vast financial empires put together on the fringes of the law, corrupt political leaders, manufacturers of hand guns and ammunition, producers of trashy movies and commercials all seem to be making it big while we live decent, hard-working lives and barely seem to make it at all.

Pious hypocrites who go to Mass every week or even every day cheat and rob and steal as soon as they are outside of the church—so, how can it be that they are rich, powerful, and happy? Why do they have long lives, expensive pleasures, fancy houses, jet-set vacations, and the best medical care that money can buy? And the ordinary honest, hard-working husband and father must work overtime or take a second job to make ends meet, cannot afford a new car, has his paycheck eroded by taxes and inflation, and can be wiped out by a sudden illness.

It is certainly not fair.

A number of modern writers have insisted that after Auschwitz it is impossible to believe in God, or at least in God's goodness. When six million people could be destroyed in gas chambers because of their religion, God must not be watching, or must not care, or perhaps does not even exist.

The problem is serious, although it did not begin with the Nazi concentration camps. Auschwitz, as terrible as it was, was by no means the first mass murder in human history. How could God have permitted any of them?

And most serious of all, how can God permit me, or anyone, to die?

So there is unfairness in the world—unfairness of opportunity, unfairness of outcome, unfairness in the reward of virtue and the punishment of evil, unfairness in the obligation to die. At first we are angry, outraged, and dismayed. We may eventually resign ourselves to the unfairness of life and learn to live with it, but we are still baffled as to why God would permit such injustice in the world.

Yet there are times when we glimpse the possibility that justice will be done. Sometimes the evil get caught and are punished. Occasionally virtue is recognized and rewarded. We know that such judgments are not permanent (both the evil and the virtuous will die) or universal (many of the evil go unpunished); but still we recognize that in our own hunger for justice and our own outrage over its absence we are stubbornly clinging to "oughtness"; people "ought" to be good, those who ignore the imperatives of ethical responsibility "ought" to be punished. If pressed as to where this "oughtness" comes from, it is hard for those of us who are not ethical philosophers to answer. (It is also difficult for the professional ethicians to answer.) There is moral obligation all right, and it seems to be built into the nature of things. But one can hardly explain the presence of "oughtness" in the world unless someone put it there. If there are laws that must be followed independently of any human lawgiver, then there must be some "force" out there that created them and that imposed their obligations. He, then, must be responsible for rendering judgment against those who violate them.

Most of us don't think about such elaborate ideas as "universal ethical imperatives," but we do perceive a demand for judgment and justice to be in the very nature of things, and hence we feel that whoever or whatever is "out there" must also be a judge.

And that is sometimes not a very comforting thought, because if there is a judge, then he will sit in judgment of us.

The Hebrew predecessors of Jesus were greatly concerned about justice. Yahweh laid great demands on them and punished them severely if they were unfaithful to him. But he had promised them an inheritance as numerous as the sands of the desert. Would he live up to his promise? In the later Hebrew religion, when Yahweh was perceived as dealing, not just with the corporate person but with individual human beings, the question of justice became even more agonized. The Hebrews saw that the evil prospered and the good suffered. Doubtless the evil persons would die for their sins, but then so, too, would the good die despite their virtue. Where was the justice in that?

The classic description of the problem is found in the Book of Job. That good but confused man has done everything a man could possibly do, and he still finds himself punished. His friends taunt him with the observation that he must be a sinner since only the evil are punished, but Job knows he is being treated unfairly and complains to Yahweh. Much to Job's dismay, Yahweh himself appears on the scene and gives him an answer:

"Who is this obscuring my designs with his empty-headed words? Brace yourself like a fighter; now it is my turn to ask questions and yours to inform me. Where were you when I laid the earth's foundations? Tell me, since you are so well-informed! Who decided the dimensions of it, do you know? Or who stretched the measuring line across it? What supports its pillars at their bases? Who laid its cornerstone when all the stars of the morning were singing with joy, and the Sons of God in chorus were chanting praise? Who pent up the sea behind closed doors when it leapt tumultuous out of the womb, when I wrapped it in a robe of mist and made black clouds its swaddling bands; when I marked the bounds it was not to cross and made it fast with a bolted gate? Come thus far, I said, and no farther: here your proud waves shall break.

Have you ever in your life given orders to the morning or sent the dawn to its post, telling it to grasp the earth by its edges and shake the wicked out of it, when it changes the earth to sealing clay and dyes it as a man dyes clothes; stealing the light from wicked men and breaking the arm raised to strike?" Job 38:2–15. It is a shattering answer. "This is my universe, Job, not yours. I made it, I know how to run it. I created the ethical imperative from which comes your hunger for fairness, and I damn well know how to enforce it. Don't try to tell me how to run my world."

It is a very tough answer, and at one level it is the only answer we are ever going to get. That God has a plan we are prepared to believe, but the designs of the plan are beyond our comprehension.

However, Yahweh gave another response to the question, and the name of that response was Jesus.

The followers of Jesus discovered justice in the Christ event. In the resurrection of Jesus, God proved himself a just and fair God. He had validated the claims made in his name by the good man who was his son. He did not permit the tomb to have domination over Jesus. Unfairness was put to rout, and the right balance of things was restored. The Christ event was an ethical experience, an experience of justice being rendered, of righteousness being exercised, of goodness being vindicated. The early Christian writers were filled with this sense of justification and vindication, and wrote with an exultation about God's judgment, which we who have been raised in the "day of wrath" tradition of the judging God cannot understand. We are afraid of God's fiery, judging wrath. Our predecessors seemed to rejoice in it. We are not sure that we are with the sheep instead of the goats. They seemed to have little doubt in the matter.

But they were closer to the Christ event and understood this aspect of it far better than we do. They experienced the judging God as a God of grace who revealed himself in Jesus. In the resurrection of Jesus the forces of evil were put to flight, and by God's grace we were united with Jesus. The judging God was the one who leaned over backward to forgive even before forgiveness was asked. Mercy and judgment were not in conflict; mercy had been extended to humankind, the forces of evil were being dispersed. Unfairness was driven from the earth, and with the coming of grace we were awarded fairness in superabundance. We were no longer in the position of Job who could complain about what was taken away from him; God had given us something so beyond our wildest fantasies that we had no complaints at all. We had already won everything.

In moments of intense religious experience such an insight into the fairness of God was enough. You don't ask someone why he is not fair when he has just given you everything he has. Still there are, as the journalists say, many unanswered questions. Are the good rewarded and the just punished in the life that survives death? Jesus certainly alluded to both possibilities during his ministry. He was going to the Father to prepare a place for his followers. There was room for many different kinds of people there—there were many mansions. In our wildest imaginings we could not dream how splendid it would be. On the other hand, it was possible to be cut off from God and to lose the great rewards; we could be plunged into a pit of fire from which we could never escape. The "fire" references are thought by most Scripture commentators today to be part of the apocalyptic rhetoric of the era in which Jesus lived, but there is no doubt about the threat of being cut off. The grace of God was offered, it was not forced upon us. We could refuse to be united with him, and that refusal could be permanent at death. But the refusal was our choice, not

God's. We condemned ourselves. His judgment on individual persons was one of loving mercy; our judgments of ourselves could take a different course.

But Jesus was quite guarded in his comments on the after-life. Unlike many other religious founders, he did not go into any great detail about either the joys of heaven or the pains of hell. Hence the imagination of Christians filled in the details with superabundant richness. We should distinguish carefully between the revelation in Jesus and the work of Christian imagination. From the former, about all we know is that God wills for us eternal happiness, and that we can refuse to accept the gift and cut ourselves off from him. God establishes his fairness by giving us our wildest dream; but by leaving us free to turn away from it, he gives us a choice. We can have eternal life if we want it; we can rise from the dead as Jesus did, but only if we unite ourselves with Jesus. Perfection in this union is not demanded, and we are readily forgiven when we err, but we still must respond to the gift. Eternal life, Jesus tells us, is about love and about freedom in response to love.

Beyond that, Jesus is modest and reserved about details. We cannot imagine how good things will be, so, in effect, we are told we shouldn't try. We will live, and that is enough.

And it is the life that we have here on earth that will continue. We will not survive death as some sort of depersonalized life force or a shadowy soul cut off from the body. The immortality of the soul was a Greek philosophical concept that was foreign to Hebrew religious thought. The early Hebrews knew of Sheol, in which the shades of the dead continued, but these shades were not the real persons. You were not yourself without your body. So the later Hebrew thinkers concluded that Yahweh's love must involve survival of the individual person and they spoke, not of the survival of the "soul," an idea that they could not grasp, but of the resurrection of the body. It was resurrection that Jesus preached, not immortality. The whole person survives and not just a ghost. The body, like the soul, was saved by Jesus, so the body must also enjoy the triumph of Jesus.

The details are not provided—much to the joy of theologians, who have agonized over them ever since. We do not know how that part of the human person that survives death continues to relate to the body or to the material world until the time when all bodies and souls are reunited.

We have no notion of how the blessed will occupy themselves throughout eternity (though some works of Christian piety make their existence sound dreadfully dull). We simply know that they will be alive. We do not know what the unblessed will do; in fact we do not know whether in the long run there will be any unblessed. We do not know for a fact that there is any human in hell. If the details were not provided, the reason must be that they were not considered to be important. Heaven and hell are presented as realities that demand a choice, and it is the choice that is important, not the details of what comes after it. We must either ally ourselves with the passionately loving goodness that animates the universe and freely offers itself to us or run the risk of being cut off from that love. Wild imaginings about the details may do no great harm, but they should not distract us from the critical challenge of the choice.

The blessed will be alive and active. As far as images go, the everlasting fish fry of Marc Connelly's *Green Pastures* is probably as good as any.

Contemporary Catholic writers note very carefully that heaven and hell are very different kinds of realities. (Hence this question is concerned with the mystery of heaven and not with the mystery of heaven and hell.) Heaven is a certainty, hell only a possibility. God came that we might have life, and have it we shall. The gift of God's loving goodness will be accepted and responded to at least by some—about that there can be no doubt at all. Will it be rejected in the final moment by some (wherever and whenever that moment may be)? The possibility of such rejection cannot be denied; human freedom requires that the possibility remains open. Whether in fact it has ever been rejected is something that we simply do not know, nor do we have any right to draw limitations on how far the divine generosity can go. The good will be rewarded, the evil punished; but whether there will be at the end any evil at all is a matter about which we know nothing. More important is the fact that as long as we live there is for us the possibility of rejecting the divine gift. Such a possibility—and it must be a real one for freedom to mean anything at all—is far more important than academic debates about what may have happened to the great villains of history.

The Christian believes in life. It was life that triumphed in the resurrection. He believes in superabundant, gracious, never-ending life. She believes, as G. K. Chesterton put it, that life is far too important to ever be anything but life. And because he believes in life, he lives confidently. He is afraid of death because he is human, but the fear does not paralyze him or turn him into a cautious naysayer. She takes her chances and she lives. He does not like the unfairness in the world, and he does not understand it. But he knows that we will all be treated fairly ultimately because all of us have been given a chance at a life that is too important to ever be anything but life.

So he lives with hope and with fear, caught between the possibility of heaven and hell; but he lives bravely and openly with an expectation of resurrection. In John Shea's words, "As for that death which all men move toward hesitantly, perhaps the most useful virtue man can take with him is a capacity for surprise."

THEOLOGICAL NOTE

Our acceptance of the grace of God's love is always hesitant and imperfect. We know from the Scripture that the imperfection of our union with God is not held against us. But still it does not seem unreasonable to believe that some kind of final preparation may be necessary to perfect our acceptance of the gift before we receive its fullness. The Catholic doctrine of purgatory conveys both the fact of our imperfection and the presumed possibility of some final preparation. The where and the what of purgatory are beyond our knowledge, of course. It is important to note, however, that it is a doctrine of mercy and not of judgment. As Jesus insisted over and over again, divine justice is mercy.

Chapter Twelve

The Mystery of the Return of Jesus

Will we ever find peace?

(When will the Last Judgment occur?)

Wᴇ ᴀʟʟ ᴅʀᴇᴀᴍ ᴏꜰ ᴘᴇᴀᴄᴇ, ᴏꜰ ᴀ ᴛɪᴍᴇ ᴡʜᴇɴ ʜᴜᴍᴀɴᴋɪɴᴅ can live together in justice, friendship, abundance, and tranquillity. In ancient times there was a hope of the return of the Golden Age when the father God (Kronos or Saturn) was awake, and the gods and humans shared the world in harmony with each other. There had been such a time once; perhaps it would return again—one knew not how. The Hebrews shared this dream with their pagan neighbors. Once there had been paradise, and the messianic age would come when the lamb and the lion would lie down together, when the hungry would be fed, the blind given sight, and the lame the power to walk, and when a great banquet table would be set up and all the nations would come to eat around it.

Paradise was more a hope for the future than it was an historical account of the past. It fed the hopes of humankind instead of appeasing their intellectual interests. The paradise hope continued into the Middle Ages, when prophets would announce the coming of a new age of the world the Third Age or the Age of the Holy Spirit. In the last century, secular versions of it appeared. The South Sea Islands became an imagined paradise for the sober, respectable bourgeoisie of London and Paris. The classless society of the socialists offered a paradise for the workers, as did the anarchists' symbolic Day of the General Strike. The dream of a world court, world law, and world parliament stirred the hopes of liberal rationalists, which led first to the League of Nations and then to the United Nations—world bodies that would prevent war. Recently the vision of the "greening of America," of a collapse of the artificialities of industrialism and a return to natural harmonies, impelled some young people to leave the cities and form rural communes in preparation for the new age of the world.

The hopes, the dreams, the visions of paradise have often been the products of sick and demented minds; but the appeal of these visions and the appeal of less mad prophets come from the fact that, sick or well, he who dreams of a better, more peaceful existence speaks to a longing that is deep in the human personality. We want peace, we want justice, we want honesty, we want to be in harmony with nature, our fellows, ourselves.

We know that things are not the way they should be with humankind. We may think that they were once different, but, more importantly, we would like to hope that they can be different at some time in the future. We struggle with one another and with the forces of nature. Husband does battle with wife, parents with children, brother with brother, friend with friend. There is injustice, oppression, fear, misery; and much of the injustice is based on fear. We cannot let the others have power because they may destroy us. We are not so much fighting to preserve our rights and privileges; we are fighting for our lives.

So we erect concentration camps and gas chambers; commit mass murders and assassinations; manufacture and use Saturday night specials; pass discriminatory laws; perpetuate racial and ethnic hatred; we indulge our class, sexual, and religious biases; exploit someone else's resources; we passively accept bad housing, poor education, inadequate food, and inferior medical care. We foster group hatred and collective guilt. And in defense of all these evils we maintain that we must have them for our own survival.

Still we slog ahead, hoping for something better, and thankful for whatever progress has been made. The Black Death is gone; the Spanish Influenza is less destructive; cholera, smallpox, and polio are under control. There is some measure of arms control, and there has not yet been an all-out nuclear war. Fish are swimming in the Hudson and the Thames once more, and Lake Erie has come alive again. Some things do get better. But the Ice Age may return, the earthquake will certainly hit San Francisco, and a really bad summer could produce serious famine in many parts of the world.

There are some scholars and historians who think they discern a steady path of progress in the human condition, but evolutionary optimism is not as popular now as it once was. Perhaps humankind is making progress still; in some scientific and technical and even ethical matters the progress is beyond question. But the pace of progress is slow, the path erratic, and the setbacks frequently disastrous. More recently some people have denied the optimistic vision completely, largely because of a loss of faith in science and technology. They argue that unless we return to lives of prescientific frugality and simplicity we will destroy the world and ourselves with it. Apparently, such apocalyptic doom is not supported by the best scientific evidence, but it indicates merely another search for paradise, one to be found not by progress but by a return to the past.

We dream of a new and better and more peaceful world obtained by either progress or a return to the past, or perhaps some combination of the two. Something is desperately wrong with the present world, yet it still contains some grounds for hope and expectation. We only take the dreams of a new world seriously because we think it not impossible to reach such a world from the one in which we now find ourselves.

We are conscious of the fierce battle that goes on between good and evil, fear and trust, growth and decline, love and hate, life and death. We are caught up in this battle; it goes on inside us as well as outside. The outcome is in doubt. The forces of darkness are very strong, but thus far they have not been quite strong enough. The forces of light have proved remarkably—perhaps unaccountably—resilient.

But what, we ask ourselves, is the fight all about? Why is there such a fight? Who are the contesting parties? Who will win? Is there any plan at all? Are we spending a lot of time fighting with people who should be our friends? Can we find out which way the action is going and flow along with it? When will it all end?

The powers involved have always seemed superhuman. When one looks at the disasters which have afflicted the United States since 1963, one is strongly tempted to see the designs of an evil genius—assassinations, riots, Vietnam, inflation, recession, Watergate, and September 11, 2001. Taken together they represent either a string of very bad luck or a plot. Ordinary and mediocre individuals like Hitler and Stalin can seize power and work evil far beyond the strength of their own personalities. Whole societies (like South Africa perhaps) can pass the point of no return and become fated for bloody disaster despite the best efforts of countless individuals. The evils of the slave trade still affect the United States more than one hundred years after the Emancipation Proclamation. Caught in a nuclear arms race we pile up tools of destruction that could wipe out humankind many times over. Good men do evil things out of pride, ignorance, patriotism, fear, or misunderstanding. Some of our best thought-out social reforms make things worse instead of better. The forces of darkness may not be personified, but they seem to be superhuman.

And yet there is goodness. The processes of nature go on, peace follows war, understanding increases, reconciliation is still possible, some problems are solved, some justice is achieved, some ignorance is dispelled. The forces of light are themselves pretty strong.

Most of our ancestors did not hesitate to personify the powers of light and the powers of darkness that seemed to contend for control of their world and the dominance of their lives. A popular explanation of the conflict was called "dualism." The world was the scene of combat between the forces of two gods, the god of good and the god of evil. There were flaws in the explanation, but it seemed to fit a lot of the data pretty well. Even today one finds the same attempt to separate the powers of light from the powers of darkness, and where there are no longer angels and devils there are good guys and bad guys, and some people forget that most of us are in between.

The followers of Jesus thought that in the resurrection experience they learned the meaning of the plan behind the battle. They didn't have all the details, they didn't know the "why," but they did know the goal and they saw the outcome. In the Christ event they saw that Jesus was the beginning of the messianic age (as he himself had quite explicitly claimed to be in his first public sermon in the synagogue at Capernaum, where he applied the Isaian prophecies about the blind, the sick, the deaf, and the lame to himself). They believed Jesus was the beginning of a new paradise, a new Eden. They believed that the plan of God was the gift of himself to all his creatures in his love, and that the plan would be carried to its ultimate fulfillment through Jesus. When the plan was finished Jesus would return, and he and his followers would enjoy happiness together forever.

Knowing the design and outcome of God's plan, the early Christians were less interested than we might be in the reason for this particular plan and the various forces that were at work. Why God should operate in the fashion he did is as unanswerable as the other question (which is, in fact, the same question) of why there is anything at all. Nor did they pretend to know what evil really was or why it had so much power. They paid some rhetorical attention to the issue of angels and demons, so popular with their contemporaries, but this was more to insist that these powers were subject to God and to his son than to fill out details of angelologies and demonologies. The early Christians knew that the core of the plan was the loving generosity of God and that such generosity would have the final victory. From their viewpoint the speculative details were not very important.

Could there be peace? Of course, but only when humans, strengthened by having accepted the grace of God revealed in Jesus, could trust one another enough to put aside their fears and begin to work with one another as brothers and sisters in Christ Jesus. War and violence came from fear. In the great sacrament that is Jesus we discover that fear is not necessary; we become free to trust and to love. If pushed, the early Christians would not have been narrow about it: trust and love are essential for peace, and if you have enough of those qualities in the world without knowing Jesus, you can have peace without him; but love and trust are rare indeed in the human condition, and Jesus offers the best grounds humankind has ever had for risking itself in such vulnerable ways of being in the world.

The Christian vision of what is going on in the world is caught between two sets of polar tensions. The first is the "already-not yet" tension; the plan is fully revealed in Jesus but not yet completely achieved. We know how it will end but not when or after what process. The kingdom of God is in our midst but it is also hidden in the mists of the future. Love and trust will win in the end, but we don't know what it will take to accomplish that victory.

Even more delicate is the tension between human activity

and God's fulfillment, between what will be accomplished in this world and what will happen in the final fulfillment of the plan by the action of God himself. Obviously, as followers of Jesus, we must do all we can to see that the reign of love and trust spreads upon the earth, realizing how hard the work is and how slow the progress must be. Just as obviously, the complete fulfillment of the plan depends on God, not us. But it is not clear how our efforts shade over into the divine fulfillment, how much peace we can achieve through our work, and how the fulfillment of the promise of peace will depend on the final intervention of God. In practice the question is not so important. We must commit ourselves completely to the work of the planting while we understand that God will give the harvest.

The Christian who has experienced once again the event of Easter has no doubt that Easter is a promise, a down payment on a fulfillment that is yet to come, and that the Easter peace is a peace destined for all humans. He therefore works with all his power and with both confidence and realism for that peace that is so profoundly involved in God's plan. The world is not the way it should be or could be; but someday it will be, and the power to work that transformation is already among us. It is the power of loving graciousness revealed by Jesus and reflected in our actions toward our fellow humans. Transforming the world's social structures so that they reflect such loving graciousness is not for the simple, the impatient, the neurotically enthusiastic, or the naive; but it is the work of everyone who is an adult and mature follower of Jesus.

Being a witness to the plan does not mean high-pressure salesmanship. It does mean, as Cardinal Suhard put it several decades ago, to engage in propaganda. It means rather living your life in such a way that you would be deemed a fool if Jesus were not the revelation of what life is about. Some of us are called by the Spirit who calls to transform the social and economic structures of the world; others are called to roll back the forces of ignorance, misery, and malice by the exercise of our professional talents; others serve the brothers and sisters of the Lord by performing the simple tasks that keep society running; and still others exercise the responsibility to loving witness in educating the young or providing the constant daily care they need in the home. All of us are called to generosity in our intimate relationships with those at our work, in our neighborhoods, and in our homes. Being a Christian is not something distinct from the everyday tasks that are part of work and family life. It does not mean doing special things. It means doing everything in a special way. We transform the world through our work, not merely by the work we do, though that is important, but by the way we work; we transform human relations, not merely by caring for others, though we must do that, but by caring for them with tenderness, sensitivity, and self-giving love.

The Christian faith in the working out of God's plan has always been embodied in the conviction that some day Jesus will return. Those who were present at the original Easter experience knew Jesus personally; they had walked the streets of Jerusalem and climbed the hills of Galilee with him. They missed him. In Jesus' farewell conversations with them he promised they would meet again. Caught as they were in the apocalyptic categories of their time, they frequently (though not exclusively) linked this "meeting once again" with the destruction of the world in an outburst of signs and wonders of cosmic chaos. But they knew that the important fact about the return would not be such spectacles but the return of Jesus to finish what he had begun. Faith in this return was faith that God would fulfill his promise and accomplish his plan no matter what happened. Jesus is the plan. We know that Jesus will return because we know that God's grace will triumph and that love and trust will finally transform the world into a place of peace.

We obviously do not know how any of these things will come about. A later age of Christians turned the early Church's perspective on the return of Jesus upside down. The *Parousia* (as the Greeks called it) was now not a day of fulfilled promise, of triumph and victory, so much as it was a day of wrath and terror, not a day of fulfillment of love and trust but one of righteous punishment, not a day of ultimate merciful graciousness but one of frightening retribution. The Last Judgment painting on the walls of the Sistine Chapel may be great art, but the early Christians would have thought it very bad theology because it emphasized the rhetoric and forgot the substance of the Second Coming—or at least it distracted from that substance. When Jesus comes again, it will not be a day of wrath but a day of joy. It will be the Easter event once again, this time for all to experience directly. The reality that was present in the promise of Easter will be present in its totality. The loving goodness of God will have been finally extended to us in its complete, wild, passionate graciousness. That is why Christians pray with St. John in the last word of the Scriptures, "Come, Lord Jesus."

In the meantime we continue to work in the world, not fully understanding the obscure cosmic processes in which we are caught up but confident that we know how they will end. We are not rose-spectacled optimists thinking that everything will be all right if there were only some changes in the social and economic systems or in child-rearing practices; but neither are we prophets of doom who expect humankind to destroy itself, despairing of improvement in the shape of human society and human culture. We work while we have light, confident that even when our light is extinguished it will only be temporary. We are confident, too, that the "light has come into the world, and darkness will not be able to put it out."

THEOLOGICAL NOTE

Theologians are not sure whether belief in the personality of angels is necessary to the Christian faith. There are forces of good (and evil) in the world that go beyond the individual human. These forces are subjected to God and to God's plan as revealed in Jesus. The forces of goodness do God's bidding and are his agents. Whether they are distinct from him and exist as separate creatures is not clear; neither is it clear that the Scriptures or the official documents of the Christian tradition wish to insist strictly on the existence of angels as separate creatures. However, belief in angels is hardly a point for one to get hung up over. Most Christians would probably conclude that it would be rather nice for there to be angels.

Also most Christians are offended by such exploitation of superstition as contained in movies like *The Exorcist*. Doubtless evil is very powerful; but if these powers are personified, surely they have better things to do than to take over the bodies of eleven-year-old girls so as to make them shout obscene words and engage in vulgar actions. Evil is much more terrible than the trivialities that such superstitious obsessions would suggest.

Conclusion

THIS CATECHISM HAS ASSUMED THAT RELIGION STANDS midway between ethics and philosophy. Like philosophy it deals with the ultimate issues of human existence; like ethics it provides a program for life. But unlike philosophy it is not concerned with speculative or abstract questions; it rather attempts to be concrete and practical, to create experiences of the "Other" so that in such experiences people can understand "in the flesh" what life means *for them*. Unlike ethics religion does not offer a detailed list of "oughts" and "ought nots," but rather a more general yet nonetheless very concrete "ought" of how one should orient oneself toward the world, the self, and other human beings. Doing or not doing certain things is not religion; religion is a way of doing everything.

Religion is not, however, anti-intellectual. The religious believer has some very clear and unpoetic ideas about what the world and human life mean. She may express these ideas in poetic imagery to give them more power, but the ideas are themselves quite specific. (In fact, the process is usually the other way around, both personally and historically: one draws out the interpretation by reflecting on the images.)

We have seen in this catechism that the Christian believes that the world and human life are good rather than evil, purposeful rather than random, loving rather than arbitrary. He believes that death is not the end of human existence, that human nature is basically good (though it is caught in a trap of sinfulness), that human society is intended to be supportive rather than oppressive, and that nature can and must be used with respect and reverence because it is "grace," a sacrament of God's love. He believes that we can be saved from evil and, in fact, that we have been. He argues that we can run the risk of trusting ourselves to others in intimate love because we live in a context of protective trust. He believes that the basic design of our existence is a love affair in which a passionately generous Other has given himself totally to us and demands total giving in return. He believes that this Other is both active and dominant, as well as tender and seductive, and that the Other calls for that which is most generous and most creative in our own personalities. He believes that human beings respond to the offer of loving goodness, not as isolated, atomized individuals but as members of a human community who support one another and look toward the reunification of the whole of humanity. He believes that no matter how powerful evil may be it is not quite powerful enough to conquer good. He believes that the world can be made a more human place in which to live, and that he is called to devote his life to this humanization, especially by reflecting in his relations with others the loving, self-giving service with which the Other has given himself to us.

This set of beliefs constitutes a quite explicit, specific, and consistent view of the meaning of human existence. It is theoretical in the sense of providing a pattern for human living, but it is not theoretical in the sense of having been philosophized about. It is not ethics, because it does not yet contain any specific moral imperatives, but it demands a style of life that is far more of a challenge to human generosity than any specific imperative could possibly be.

Let no one say that such a "theory" of life is merely a matter of psychology. It surely resonates with some of the insights of psychological research. How could a valid theory of life fail to resonate with human search for truth? It also represents a set of convictions that would underwrite a psychologically healthy existence if they were true. But the propositions that constitute the Christian theory are not self-evidently true, nor are they provable by either the research or the theory of the social sciences. All psychology can say is that in their better moments most humans would rather like to believe the theory is true and indeed have received hints that it might well be. On the other hand, the data are ambiguous, and human skepticism finds such a brightly hopeful theory of life too good to be true.

Hence one finally accepts or rejects the Christian theory of life only by a leap of faith. It might very well be true; but on the other hand, it might not. The only way to achieve practical certainty is to "try the theory on," to live it for a while and see if the world experienced from the perspective of such a commitment is a kind of world worth living in, worth hoping for, worth loving. The theory may still seem too good to be true, but as we live it, we may come to see its truth.

So the theory presented in this catechism is ultimately the object of faith. However strange the language and the method of this book may seem to those educated in other catechetical styles, there is no attempt here to eliminate faith from religion. If anything, it is harder to accept than the theory presented in other catechetical methods. Some other forms of Christian education are content with the intellectual acceptance of certain doctrinal propositions and the honoring of certain moral imperatives (usually negative). This catechism argues that such behavior is rather easy, or at least not too difficult. But Christianity demands more than intellectual acceptance of certain propositions. It demands that the total person embrace a theory that gives a complete description of the meaning of human life, and then that the person live that theory in his daily existence. It also demands much more than the performance or nonperformance of certain behavior; it demands from us a style of loving generosity that will affect all our behavior. Christian faith demands total personal transformation that is much more difficult than intellectual assent or ethical purity. Fortunately for us, we are not required to be perfect in this transformation but rather to keep trying despite repeated failures.

The Catholic Christian who seeks to restate what he believes, and the non-Catholic adult who is curious about where Catholic Christianity stands should understand that there is much more about Catholicism that is not in this book. There are details of doctrine, worship, and practice that fill many volumes. Some of these details are fascinating, others are important, others are useless but mildly interesting. (For example, what is the proper title for a cardinal? In German, *Herr Kardinal*; in Italian, *Signor Cardinale*; in French, *Monsieur le Cardinal*; and in English, the language of democratic freedom and equality—not Mr. Cardinal but Your Eminence.) Other details are colossal bores and are maintained to keep harmless clerks in business. (For example, the various canonical punishments listed in exquisite detail in the Code of Canon Law.) If one is to be a Catholic Christian, it may well be a help to know some or even many of these details, but they should not be confused with the essence of the Catholic Christian theory.

There are also details of all the mistakes the leadership of Catholic Christianity has made through history—the scandals which have beset the Church (and which, alas, still do), the sinfulness of the ordinary Catholic Christian, the perennial incompetence of many of his leaders. Such details, heaven knows, make for entertaining history and relieve the Catholic Christian from the necessity of expecting perfection from the human members and the human structure of his Church.

Scandals and failures however should not obscure what the Catholic Christian theory stands for; they should have nothing to do with whether one embraces the theory or not. If one wants to know whether the theory offers a life worth living, then one should look at the people who really lived it (the saints) and at those Catholics in their best moments when they are trying hard to live it.

So there are many things about Catholicism that are not in this book, but the really critical mysteries are all here, the ones that respond to the fundamental agonies of life and death that torment all humankind. Catholic Christianity begins with the experience of wonder and ends with the development of a capacity for surprise.

Guide for Discussion and Personal Meditation

Introduction

How does this catechism seem to be different from other catechisms you've seen? Does it seem to be radical?

What does it mean to say that religious action precedes rather than follows reflection? Can you think of other aspects of your life where the same thing is true?

What does *mystery* mean in this book? How does this meaning differ from other meanings of *mystery* you have heard?

Why is it important that religion be grounded in experience?

What have your experiences been of "something else" going on in the universe? When did they occur? How did they affect you?

Chapter One

What were some of the wonder experiences in your life? When did they happen? What impact did they have on you? Why do you think you don't have more of them?

What is your "daily" picture of God, your "working image" of God? What kind of a world does a God like that reveal to you?

Why are we afraid to admit that God might be passionately in love with us?

Does the interpretation of the story of the "crazy farmer" shock you? Do you think God could really be like the crazy farmer? Or the permissive father who spoiled the prodigal son?

Why do so many people seem to prefer a God of justice to a God of love?

Chapter Two

What were the times in life when you have experienced the strongest hope? What was it like? How did it start? How do you feel now about such experiences?

Why does our hopefulness diminish so quickly? Why do so many people refuse to believe the "hint of an explanation" that hope gives them?

What does it mean to live in the time between the "already" and the "not yet"?

What does it mean to say: "If Jesus were certain, he would not be one of us"?

What is the Jerusalem to which you must go up? How will you go?

Chapter Three

What were your greatest moments of trust and openness? When did they happen? How did you react? How long did they last? What happened afterwards?

Why do we so fearfully pull back from trust?

Why is marriage the intimate relationship *par excellence*? Why is there so much fear and distrust in marriage?

Why is the Holy Spirit called a "dancing God"? What is special in you that the Holy Spirit tries to call forth when inviting you to the dance?

What are the risks in deceiving ourselves about the Holy Spirit? How can we tell that we are not being deceived?

Chapter Four

What are the worst personal experiences of evil you have ever had? And the best experiences of good? Which seem to you now to have been stronger?

How have you experienced death and resurrection? Deep down inside, which seemed stronger?

How does the "Christ event" illuminate the mystery of good and evil for you?

What does it mean to say that the resurrection is a sacrament? Why is the ultimate question not whether Christ rose but whether we will all rise?

What are the consequences in your own life of the mystery of the resurrection? How do you feel about these consequences?

Chapter Five

What are the worst things you do? And the best? Which is stronger in you—good or evil? Are you more good than bad or more bad than good? Under what circumstances does the evil in you seem strongest?

What are the traps in which you feel caught? What is the worst isolation you experience?

Are liberation and reconciliation really possible in your life? How can you escape the traps, break down the barriers?

How does Jesus enable us to find freedom and community?

What is the Catholic Christian view of the nature of human nature? How does it differ from other views?

Chapter Six

What are your worst feelings of guilt? Do you kid yourself about guilt, sliding over the real responsibilities and assuming phony responsibilities?

What are your feelings of forgiveness?

How strong is your feeling of self-hatred and self-rejection? Do you punish yourself even after others (God included) have forgiven you?

What does it mean to say that God is gracious? How have you experienced this grace?

What kind of graciousness must we show to others? What does it mean that loving forgiveness is contagious?

Chapter Seven

What were your closest friendships? What went wrong with these relationships? What went right? How did the friendships affect you? How would you do it over?

Why are our interludes of loving friendship usually so brief?

Why is eating together a sign of friendship?

When are our common meals the best? Why do such meals sometimes go wrong? How necessary is it to be considerate of others in order to make the common meals happy?

What does the Eucharist tell us about the possibility of friendship? Why is this meaning often not obvious in our Sunday worship?

Chapter Eight

Why are we afraid of those who are different from us? Why is there so much hatred for other groups?

Have you had any experiences in which you have discovered that the "stranger" is in fact a "brother"?

What was the program of Jesus for uniting humanity?

Why is there a Church at all? Who is the Church? Why has the Church made so many mistakes?

How does the Church point toward a vision of a reconstituted humanity? What does it mean to say that the Church is made up of servants? To what extent has the Church failed? Why?

Is there a Catholic answer to social problems?

Chapter Nine

How does the use and abuse of the environment relate to baptism?

Have you had any experiences of the power and the healing effects of water?

How is baptism a reenactment of the Christ event?

Why is the baptismal water blessed and the baptismal vows renewed on Easter?

What does it mean to say that some signs are sacraments—precisely because all material elements are gracious?

Chapter Ten

What experiences have you had of the fear of your sexuality? In what experiences has it been a revelation of grace?

Why did the Church go down the wrong track for so long on sex?

How did devotion to Mary develop in the Church?

What implications for human sexuality in the modern world does devotion to Mary really have?

What does it mean to say that God is both our powerful father and our loving mother? How is the sexual union a sacrament of the Christ event?

What does Mary's role of reflecting the femininity of God tell us about the equality of men and women?

Chapter Eleven

Why is envy such a powerful human emotion? Why do the evil prosper? Why do you have to die? What is the answer of God to Job?

What experiences have you had of the hunger for fairness?

How is Jesus a response to the search for fairness? How does the Christ event reveal God's fairness?

What do you think heaven will be like?

What does it mean to say that Christians prepare for death by developing a capacity for surprise?

CHAPTER TWELVE

What was your strongest experience of peace?

Why is peace so hard to find?

How do Christians respond to the problem of injustice and misery in the world? What is the correct answer to the charge that Christian belief in the afterlife lowers concern about righting the wrongs in this life?

What is God's game plan for the New Creation?

What does a Christian's experience of the peace of Christ have to contribute to the struggle for justice and peace among humans? What does it mean to say that Christianity does not mean doing special things but rather doing everything in a special way?

CONCLUSION

How does religion stand between ethics and philosophy?

Summarize the Christian answer to the twelve questions that are asked in this book. Is this answer encouraging?

How do you achieve practical certainty about the Christian faith?

How must you live if you believe the answer you have summarized in question 2? Is this life easy? How perfect do you have to be at it?

What does it mean to say that Christianity begins in wonder and ends with a capacity for surprise?